Design Secrets:
Office Spaces

GLOUCESTER MASSACHUSETTS

ROCKPORT PUBLISHERS

elana frankel

ROCKPORT

First published in the United States of America by
Rockport Publishers, Inc.
33 Commercial Street
Gloucester, Massachusetts 01930-5089
Telephone: (978) 282-9590
Facsimile: (978) 283-2742
www.rockpub.com

ISBN 1-56496-769-7

10 9 8 7 6 5 4 3 2 1

Design & Layout: Terry Patton Rhoads
Cover Design: Madison Design and Advertising

Printed in China.

contents

5   Introduction

6   4You Youth Bank THE UNIT
10   Agency.com HLW
14   America Online SIDMAN/PETRONE ARCHITECTS
18   AT & T HOK
22   ATTIK CHRISTOPHER ROSE
26   Axis Theatre Company MESSANA O'RORKE ARCHITECTS
30   Bang & Olufsen KHRAS
34   barnesandnoble.com ANDERSON ARCHITECTS
38   Bates Advertising STUDIOS
42   Blue Hypermedia SPECHT HARPMAN
46   CarsDirect.com GENSLER
50   Click3XLA PUGH & SCARPA
54   Clickthings FOX & FOWLE
58   Condé Nast MANCINI DUFFY
62   Coolsavings.com PARTNERS BY DESIGN
66   Digital Pulp DATUM/O
70   DoubleClick THE PHILLIPS GROUP
74   Eagle River Interactive D'AQUINO MONACO
78   eEMERGE NBBJ
82   EHPT LOMAR ARCHITECTS AND SCHEIWILLER SVENSSON ARCHITECTS
86   Eisner Communications GENSLER
90   Euro RSG Tatham SPACE
94   Executive Presentation Theater TVS INTERIORS
98   Fluidminds URSING ARCHITECTS' BUREAU
102   Funny Garbage SPECHT HARPMAN
106   Hill & Knowlton ORMS
110   Hurd Studios SPECHT HARPMAN
114   InternetConnect INTERIOR SPACE INTERNATIONAL (ISI)
118   ‹kpe› ANDERSON ARCHITECTS
122   Liquid Design Group FREECELL
124   NUTOPIA NUCREATIVES
128   Oxygen Media THE PHILLIPS GROUP
132   Pomegranit HOLEY ASSOCIATE

136   Predictive System, Inc. ANDERSON ARCHITECTS
140   RiskMetrics Group STUDIOS
144   Scient WILLIAM GREEN
148   Screaming Media HUT SACHS STUDIO
152   SFX Entertainment GERNER + VALCARCEL
156   SHR Perceptual Management MORPHOSIS
160   Smith Brothers Hardware RETAIL PLANNING ARCHITECTS
164   Sofinnova HUNTSMAN ARCHITECTURAL GROUP
168   Straw Dogs WILLIAM EMMERSON AND PUGH & SCARPA
172   Studio at Third Avenue GOULD EVANS ASSOCIATES
176   Thunder House RESOLUTION: 4 ARCHITECTURE
180   Upshot SPACE
184   Videoconferencing Office WILLIAM T. GEORGIS
188   Wineshopper.com HUNTSMAN ARCHITECTURAL GROUP
192   Wired Digital HOLEY ASSOCIATES
196   Zefer BARGMANN HENDRIE + ARCHETYPE (BH+A)
200   The Zone at PricewaterhouseCoopers GENSLER

204   Directory of Firms and Photography
207   About the Author
207   Acknowledgments

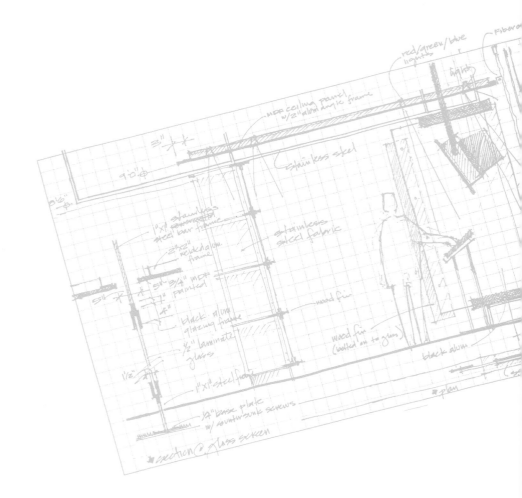

Introduction

When venture capitalists began throwing money at new high-tech start-ups in the 1990s, frenzy followed. In order to retain a much-needed, computer-savvy labor force, whose average age is 24, employers became benevolent patrons, supplying employees with such corporate phenomena as playgrounds, recreation and nap areas, and espresso-on-demand. At the same time, employees began to look for companies that would satisfy not only their professional needs but also their personal wants, including sabbaticals, in-house individual services and amenities, and even frat-like perks. Large corporations played catch-up by rebranding and retooling their business efforts and redesigning their marketing schemes to appeal to the new e-generation.

Couple these business happenings with rising commercial real estate costs, rapid growth potential, fierce competition, and the need for speed and it instigated a corporate revolution. Dress-down Fridays were simply a rude awakening. Say goodbye to traditional cubicles, hierarchical corner offices, office paneling, and a simple water cooler/vending machine area. Instead, welcome free-form workspaces, custom workstations that are flexible and mobile, quirky architectural and design statements, full-blown cafeterias and play stations.

Today's new media businesses—Web and Internet production houses, digital designers, print- and e-publishing, and the various service support agencies—are on the cutting edge of industry, producing culturally penetrating images and fostering creativity, experimentation, and innovation and yet are still trying to define themselves. Though the stock market wavers, expectations undulate, and brokers hem and haw, the industry keeps moving forward, pushing business boundaries and dumping dated corporate ideals. And, the design industry keeps up with the creativity and chaos.

New media dictates new design ideas. These 50 projects reveal how interior designers and architects are creating user-friendly, flexible workplaces that respond to the current trends, and in most cases without breaking the bank. Looking over the shoulders of designers, who create high-tech furniture design, teaming areas, and recreation rooms, New Economy businesses are profiled in-depth. Progressive offices, both new and established, are presented and each illustrated with original plans, sketches, models, perspectives, and presentation drawings. As you will notice, corporate America can never be the same.

After lengthy discussions and meetings with the Austrian-based Kremser Bank, architects Georg Petrovic and Wolfgang Burgler, a team of young Viennese architects called The Unit, decided on one simple project goal for the 4You Youth Bank

The flower-like Netboy system gives kids an opportunity to surf the Net and enjoy interactive banking, replacing the traditional reception area. This minimalist approach is also seen in the use of concrete and glass throughout the building.

branch at Bahnhofsplatz in Krems: reduce the gap between youth culture and the banking world. The new branch had to be a meeting place for youth; a platform for communication that makes it possible for kids to approach the subject of banking. The Unit, a name that stands for an understated, purist, almost meditative style, claimed a minimalist, almost spartan approach for the bank branch. The project relies on certain strong cultural identifiers to develop the link between financial business and youth.

Instead of spending advertising dollars on a new campaign geared toward the youth market, Kremser Bank chose to filter its resources into a 2,555-square-foot (230-square-meter) space dedicated to state-of-the-art multimedia technology and kids. Nicknamed the Youth Box, the architects, with the help of project manager Peter Reindl, and assistants Michael Pfannhauser and Andreas Petrovic, first opened up the plinth area of a nondescript post-war apartment building the client chose and replaced it with a protruding transparent glass and aluminum box.

Continuing with a minimalist approach and rebelling against classical bank office design, Petrovic and Burgler did not use standard materials (lavish marble, lush upholstery, rich woods), but instead kept the original concrete floors and walls, which are not primed and painted, but roughly dabbed with a sponge, and utilized glass throughout. A seat/skating ramp emerges from the concrete floor and a computer terminal called Netboy, a multimedia touch-station to surf the Web, replace the reception area. Monitors with MTV videos flicker out across the wall and color images of larger-than-life teenagers stare out into the street.

Since the space is a bank, a cash station and bank statement printer do make an appearance. The marketing agenda is pretty obvious, but there are no aggressive sales tactics, and bank employees, seemingly as young as the clientele, encourage kids to experiment with their own non-banking ideas. The client's established motto is: "Don't Push." There is a separate and discreet room that can be used for opening up accounts or getting more bank information. Financial workshops and informational meetings are held in the facility and kids can access the bank's homepage on any of the computers to receive tips or counseling, talk in a chat room about movies, music, or even hook up with a blind date.

From the interior, the façade of teenage images continue their stare. A concrete seat/skateboard ramp invites kids to do what they like best—play. The original concrete floors and walls were kept from the old building, roughly dabbed with a sponge.

The exterior façade of the 4YOU Youth Bank is a protruding glass and aluminum box that invades the sidewalk. The startling visual effect, coupled with the larger-than-life images of teenagers, leads potential visitors to take a second look.

A second floor, fitted only with a couch, a multimedia Globe station, and PC terminals, which were designed by the architects themselves, is a clear message to teenagers. Here they can edit videos, copy music, or surf the Web. The project's unofficial theme, "streetball meets banking future," is played out by a street ball pitch that is painted on the floor. A sliding wall has a graffiti-painted vinyl netting material that stretches on a frame and is mounted on rollers. During the daytime, light filters through and at night, it obstructs the view. This sliding wall appears again throughout the space as a neutral glass wall to the bank room and as a red-colored sliding wall that conceals the cloakroom and condom machine. Clearly the architectural design team has devised a space for teenagers to hang out, have fun, and learn about banking under the auspices of clean, minimalist design.

With a budget of 12 million Austrian schillings and the help of the Viennese-based multimedia consultants Fast Forward Group, the design team reduced the space to its essentials and focused on state-of-the-art multimedia technology to build a brand identity and commercial setting. This includes a large-format video beamer, audio equipment, Internet access, and computer workstations for editing videos—all of which have mass appeal to its target audience. For Petrovic and Burgler, the space is ultimately one that is first and foremost an exciting setting that combines function and communication in architecture. They continue to recognize 4You Youth Bank as not just a marketing ploy but "a playground with street character, an emotional space, reflecting the feelings and experience of contemporary youth." And, all the while, The Unit was able to maintain their design standards and integrity.

⊗ Minimalism dominates the first-floor design as this overall shot portrays. A lone Netboy stands among the dimly lit, gray room with an inconspicuous cash machine and printer.

⊗ In order to appeal to the client's target audience, the architects combined the latest in high-tech offerings with a street ball playing field on the second floor.

A recurring theme in The Unit's design, the red door hides a cloakroom and condom machine as visitors wind their way to the second floor. This minimal design appears again as a neutral glass wall to the bank room.

The story of Agency.com could be told as yet another tale of two guys and a Mac making it big. But that would be missing the point.

In 1995, CEO Chan Suh was fresh from helping launch *Vibe Online* as director of marketing for *Time*'s hip-hop magazine, and Kyle Shannon, Chief Creative Officer, a former actor, was publishing the webzine *Urban Desires* with his wife, Gabriel Shannon. The two began Agency.com with a bigger vision than most of the Internet agencies that soon cropped up to create brochureware for the Web. They wanted to help other companies bring their businesses online. While seemingly obvious and simple now, back then this idea was nothing short of radical.

An early client who embraced this vision was British Airways, who hired the company in 1996 for a redesign of their site. Over the years, similar projects followed for other clients with familiar names like Compaq, Nike, Sprint, and Texaco. Agency.com quickly needed to expand and the result was a relationship with Omnicom, an international holding company that formed an interactive services unit called Communicade and bought a number of interactive companies, including a 40 percent share of Agency.com.

On the heels of expansion, Agency.com retained the New York City-based architecture firm HLW to create corporate offices in Cambridge, Massachusetts. After a successful completion of the offices in 1999, HLW was asked to further develop a cohesive facility design standard to be articulated in the company's Manhattan-based world headquarters and in offices worldwide. With the philosophy of the Cambridge workspace on hand—promoting learning and knowledge sharing in a team-oriented environment that embraces change and encourages innovation—HLW accepted. Since the client is one that plans to continue revolutionizing strategic Internet advertising consulting services with the latest electronic and digital technology, the project soon became a test in designing a facility with new standards in flexibility and user-friendliness—two buzzwords that could easily been seen as design clichés. But Kimberly Harvey, the project's designer, was on top of things and with HLW's scope of services including architecture, interior design, MEP engineering, structural engineering, and lighting, she was able to provide a holistic approach that fit the bill.

◈ Top: Using bright, punchy colors and an open, airy design scheme to reflect the client's corporate philosophy, the main reception area welcomes visitors to Agency.com's worldwide headquarters.

◈ Bottom: Each floor has a "town center" outfitted with a more casual teaming area for group brainstorming meetings. Vibrant, egg-shaped cushions encourage creativity and convey the company's playful work environment.

◈ HLW's Kimberly Harvey created an open workspace environment that facilitates quick and efficient moves, and accommodates the distinct identities of separate work groups while supporting individual abilities.

Combining a 156,000-square-foot (14,040-square-meter) space spread out over six floors and an additional 5,000-square-feet (450-square-meters) on one tower floor to create a consistent design identity, the offices facilitate communication among employees on multiple floors. The overriding challenge was to establish an open office plan, says Harvey, which reflected the distinct identities of separate work groups while supporting individual employee personalities and abilities. HLW designed five floors of office space, an executive floor housing a suite with private offices, main reception area, and a conference room and an employee penthouse featuring cafeteria, entertainment, and recreational facilities including a Zen den. Harvey worked closely with Agency.com to establish a somewhat unique design vocabulary that expressed the company's culture and vision. She needed to respond to the company's young, creative individuals—any cookie-cutter design tactic or Dilbert-like scenario was seen as negative, she says. For quick box moves, flexible floor plates were planned to accommodate the rapidly expanding nature of the company and constant employee shift. This was accomplished through the creation of office space that is 90 percent open on the interior surrounded by "neighborhood centers" or 6-foot-by-8-foot (1.8-meters-by-2.4-meters) workstation clusters on the exterior. Nestled in the neighborhoods, each has a "town center" equipped with a library, brainstorming room or teaming area, and support areas that contribute to the corporate culture and reflect the nature of the company's service.

Open communication and dialogue are encouraged among the many corridors that connect workspaces by the use of cork cladding on columns for employees to display their work, as well as floor-to-ceiling blackboards and whiteboards along the hallway walls and doors.

Both Agency.com management and employees were adamant about wanting a unique work environment that would not rely on previous corporate design formulas. The open layout of the office allows employees to view different areas of the office at a glance, such as the Zen den with its colorful cushions and stones.

Harvey elaborated on the company's productive and playful work environment and facilitated the communication concept by designing public areas and corridors with interconnecting stairs on the north side of the floor plan. Connecting all three employee work floors, the stairs are surrounded by a main zone, public space, and large seating area next to a pantry. Employee interaction and networking is encouraged in these common areas. Design elements that foster communications are integrated throughout the facility, such as cork cladding on columns so employees can display their work and personal expressions, and floor-to-ceiling blackboards and whiteboards along the hallway walls and doors, which are frequently used in brainstorming sessions.

Other design elements include floating "amoeba-like" ceilings and custom-designed lighting fixtures that speak to the non-traditional type of work provided by Agency.com. Harvey was sensitive to the company's lighting needs; since employees use computers all day long, the custom-designed fixtures emit a fairly low light level. The more adventurous use of bright, punchy colors capture the high-energy spirit of Agency.com. Most importantly, the client was eager to promote an egalitarian atmosphere. As a result, part of the penthouse space, with its outrageous views, is not dedicated to executives but to a more communal space with bar, pool table, and dining facilities. And, every so often, a jam session can be heard.

Harvey has seen a lot of design trends come and go, but she is convinced that amenities in Internet offices such as the ones in Agency.com will remain. "Often Internet office design can get cutesy," she says, "but different types of places where employees can sit back and relax, not jumping to the same solutions, works. Plus, employers want to make employees as comfortable as possible to retain good solid talent." And, she concludes, "it is rewarding for us not to use the same formulas over and over again."

⊗ The bold and dramatic staircase, which connects all floors of Agency.com's worldwide headquarters, facilitates employee interaction with other workgroups.

⊗ Each floor has an identical plan, maximizing the space and making it easier for employees to move around.

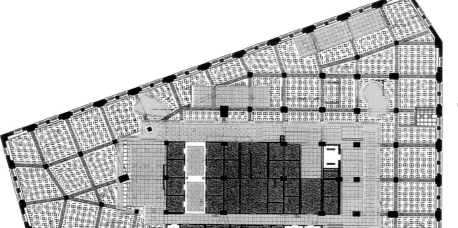

When given the right environment, a more communal atmosphere inspires everything from hard work to informal jam sessions. The Penthouse space contains a bar, pool table, and dining facilities that allow employees time away from work while still in the office.

America Online (better known to the world as AOL) commissioned Sidnam/Petrone Architects to design its **corporate offices and interactive marketing department**

(better known to the world as ad sales) in New York City, consolidating a staff that worked previously from several locations in the city. Located in Chelsea on the top floor space of a late nineteenth-century building, the facility is surrounded by superstores like Staples and Old Navy. The brick box, formerly a skylit restaurant, was on the roof of the old Siegel-Cooper department store at the corner of 6th Avenue and 18th Street, part of Ladies' Mile. During the Great War, the building was then converted into a military hospital. However, once the street was designated an historic conservation area, private developers rehabilitated the space and created retail and office spaces.

For AOL's facility, there were some criteria: create a large central gathering place for employees and social functions as well as a flexible layout. Staff from the company's Virginia headquarters are constantly making the trip up north for meetings. To meet these needs (with a modest budget by New York new media standards), the architects rendered the gathering place as well as its attendant office wings in simple materials. This made it clear that the company was putting its resources into services, not lavish offices.

Designed by William C. Petrone, the architect of record, with partners Sidnam and Eric A. Gartner and their project team, AOL's new offices are organized forum-like around a twenty-four-foot-high (7.3-meter) atrium with wood walls built from curved glulam members. The facility required new subfloors and structural modifications, new HVAC system and electrical service and distribution because of

⬡ AOL's new office is located on the top floor of a late 19th-century building in Manhattan's Chelsea district.

⬡ AOL's 16,000-square-foot (1,486-square-meter) space is divided into private and public areas.

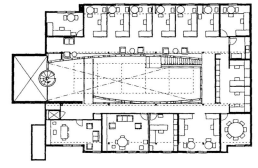

AOL-01-DS.fpo

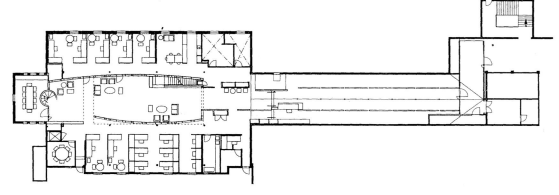

the low ceiling heights in the office wings. The architects were also confronted with an old air-raid shelter structural repair and stripping out. An existing one hundred-foot-long (30.5-meter) greenhouse structure, which connects the elevator lobby to the atrium and offices, is lined with freestanding panels of translucent Lamusite, setting the tone for the materials palette. A wood-clad reception desk transitions the entrance corridor to the offices.

The 16,000-square-foot (1,486-square-meter) space is divided into private and public areas. The offices are predicated on physical presence—sight lines, visual connections, and contained spaces. Offices and Herman Miller workstations flank the atrium on its long sides and are obscured from view by two gently curved wood-framed walls clad with perforated metal panels; coffering and metal perforations dampen sound. Depending on the vantage point and lighting conditions, the walls can appear opaque or transparent. However, the view from inside the office wings, which occupy two levels, is clear enough that employees can see one another across the atrium.

⊗ Offices with Herman Miller workstations flank the atrium on its long sides.

⊗ The atrium, featuring a living-room atmosphere for social and staff meetings, has curved and perforated metal walls. They separate the office wings from the more public areas.

⊗ A rough view looking east through the main atrium space.

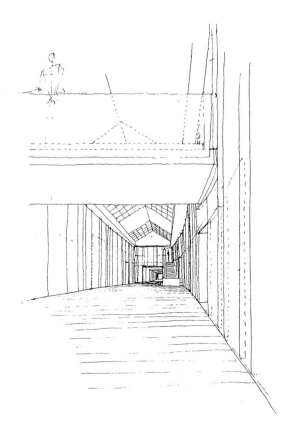

The atrium has been described as a "living room" for AOL employees to relax and discuss work issues; this is particularly advantageous to those working long shifts. This is, after all, a twenty-four-hour-a-day, seven-day-a-week operation. The mezzanine level office corridor, clad with Lumasite panels and reached from the atrium floor by a staircase clad with fiber concrete board, is furnished with lounge chairs and tables for impromptu meetings. A bridge stretches across the far end of the atrium connecting the two office wings and serves as an informal locale for quick meetings. The atrium, a self-contained space, also functions as a presentation area and is used for client-related social functions. An enclosed conference room at the far end of the atrium, furnished with Herman Miller chairs and a Vitra table, and two smaller meeting rooms in the office wings are used for more formal gatherings. An existing spiral staircase, clad with galvanized sheet metal on a wood frame leads to the conference room.

Few pieces of furniture, mostly from Palazzetti, sit on warm wood floors from Craftsman Lumber Co. and add the only bit of color. Elsewhere, finishes are simple-pine floors and white painted walls.

The design team at Sidnam/Petrone was able to fill a large, two-story space with a simple materials palette. The space gives off a sense of scale, like an interior courtyard with functional clarity and purpose, without sacrificing style.

⊗ The mezzanine level office corridor, clad with Lumasite panels, is reached from the atrium floor by a staircase clad with fiber concrete board.

⊗ A rough view looking southeast at the newly-created staircase.

An existing spiral staircase is enclosed with galvanized sheet metal on a simple wood frame. The glass doors lead to the conference room.

A bridge cuts across the width of the atrium and is clad in translucent Lumasite panels.

In 1996, New York's Hellmuth, Obata, & Kassabaum (HOK) made a competitive pitch for a building addition to the **two hundred-acre AT&T compound** in Bedminster, New Jersey

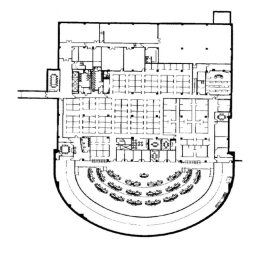

where the company has resided since 1977. The project was the AT&T Global Network Operations Center (GNOC), a leading command/control post that coordinates and manages streams of data, voice, and wireless messages sent via the company's network. Based on the company's impeccable credentials, HOK was asked to do the job. However, brainstorming sessions and idea evaluations went on almost weekly for about two-and-a-half years. When the project, led by senior principal/design director Rick Focke and representing AT&T liaison/district manager Lori Glover, finally got the go-ahead, the team was more than ready. Today, the structure stands as a testament to the power of present-day communications with plenty of visuals and graphics as well as product displays that celebrate the firm's genealogy.

The design team included HOK project manager Greg Smith, Frank Vento, Anthony Spagnolo, and Michelle Brewster, principal in charge Jerry Davis, principal for architecture Kent Turner, and principal for planning Bill Palmer, all working with a total outlay of approximately $90 million. Three extant structures, now given over to offices, predate the 200,000-square-foot (18,580-square-meter) addition. It is built on a sloping site that subsumes the two lower levels; accommodating the wholly computerized operations floor, the 70,000-square-foot (6,968-square-meter) subterranean sector can do without windows. The remaining 130,000 square feet (12,077 square meters) are for offices, reception areas, exhibitions, an Internet café, and briefing and demo centers.

The intent of GNOC was to consolidate in one place previously scattered operations managers, facilitate staff expansion, improve efficiency, and attract present and prospective customers, major stockholders, and business concerned with network communications. The operators' action area, similar to a trading floor or air traffic

⊗ Top: Shown here is one of several exhibitions in the gallery devoted to communication ideas from the past.

⊗ Bottom: The first and third floor plans are illustrated above.

⊗ The Internet Café, sited on street level, serves laptop needs.

THE AT&T GLOBAL NETWORK OPERATIONS CENTER

The operators' action area is similar to a trading floor or air traffic controllers' hub and functions as the very lifeblood of AT&T operations.

controllers' hub, functions as the very lifeblood of AT&T operations. Here the managers exercise their electronic wizardry, preventing, for example, the overloading of what used to be wires, spreading news of natural disasters, and sharing incoming information with journalists encamped in one of two media rooms. The operations centrum is equipped with one hundred forty-one 4 ft. x 5 ft. (1.2 m x 1.5 m) rear-projection screens keyed to maps, graphs, and charts; picture shows appear on a 17-foot-tall, three-hundred-thirty-five-foot-long (5.2-meter-tall, 31-meter-long) curved perimeter wall. Those in charge work in pairs at 39 custom consoles (workstation is not in the users' vocabulary). They enjoy many uncommon amenities: individually adjustable HVAC equipment, lighting, and, in a nod to ergonomics, chair positions and counter heights. Everyone has a stereo unit with speakers, television set, computer, and three flat screens. Sensors turn on and off the light when occupants arrive or leave. This workplace marvel is made of plastic laminate with steel frames and aluminum airfoil wings.

Focke's prevailing design strategy was to "see" everything through outsiders' eyes, he says. Having met by appointment in the main reception area, guests are greeted by an AT&T representative and an old-fashioned telephone pole. All advance to the Rotunda and, perhaps first drop off their luggage, clean up, and make telephone calls. Then they confront the circular chamber's riches. Looking down, they see a twenty-five-foot-diameter (7.6-meter) mosaic floor depicting a bird's-eye view of a flattened globe, the North Pole at top; ringing the map at 45-degree longitudinal intervals are eight tessellated "wind cherubs," puffing out their fat cheeks; and partially encircling the orbital wheel are glass fins vertically framing musical instruments. A Russian balalaika, French horn, Korean drum, and Scottish bagpipes symbolize the voices of communication, a theme supplemented with the widely applied "rivers and continents" motif.

Next visitors walk to the arced gallery, where individual exhibit groups dramatize objects tied to communications. Included are African "talking" drums, alluding to early ancestors of the broadcast word; an eighteenth-century quasi-mathematical puzzle having to do with topology and geographical network delineations; assemblages of vacuum tubes, loading coils, and other obsolete telephone innards; an 1840s traffic dispatch control-system used by British railroads; and a 1940s underwater cable predating satellites. Theatrical lighting brightens the route and focuses on featured items. The tour's final destination is the visitors' gallery overlooking the operational floor. Here business negotiations are reviewed and finalized.

⊘ Consoles are made of plastic laminate, steel frames, and aluminum wing tops.

⊘ In the main reception area, an old-fashioned telephone pole greets visitors.

Top and Bottom Left: The twenty-five-foot diameter (7.6-meter) mosaic floor illustrates the world map. Exhibited between glass fins are musical instruments symbolizing communications. Walls are made of pear wood.

Top Right: Technology memorabilia is displayed in a gallery that uses theatrical lighting to dramatize the scenario.

Bottom Right: The visitor's observation room has a projection screen that is lowered from the ceiling and covers the glass wall.

Before opening his own studio in 1995, San Francisco **architect Christopher Rose** got a Harvard education and more formal architecture training **by working for** Mario Botta and Santiago Calatrava.

Architect Christopher Rose gutted the building, once a former light manufacturing facility, to reveal galvanized window frames, brick walls, and high ceilings.

When asked to collaborate with company CEO Will Travis on the 4,000-square-foot office of ATTIK, one of the largest graphic design firms in San Francisco focused on digital work, including Web sites, Rose relied on all of his education to develop a new facility for a progressive and innovative client. Built in a little less than six months, the space was developed to house a staff of 20 employees, who create television commercials (think Adidas, British Telecom, and SONY), film titles, print campaigns (for the likes of Toyota and Sega), and interactive and broadcast designs. However, like many creative and high-tech firms in the 21st century, ATTIK offices now hold 32 employees and Travis is looking to expand his creative team even further.

ATTIK's building, once a former light manufacturing facility in the city's financial district, was gutted to reveal the original bones—galvanized window frames, brick walls, and high ceilings. Rose added a poured concrete floor; the management's architect enclosed the elevator lobby and bathrooms with white-painted drywall. For the space's structural and architectural elements, Rose custom developed Plexiglas and aluminum anodized walls that have wingbolts and adjustable vertical parts so they are flexible and can easily be moved (for future growth plans).

With only two sets of walls, the ATTIK space is divided between the reception area and the workspace as well as a row of conference or break-out rooms. The delineating and segmented wall was conceived as a ribbon of translucency that wraps and edges the various rooms as it flows through the existing office shell forming a bar/reception area, meeting and work areas with matching furniture. Fabricated and installed by the architect, the wall elements are made up of anodized aluminum tube and angle sections that hold in place a series of jalousie type acrylic panels and alternate in color and translucency. Reflecting the client's desire for a work environment that would convey a sense of lightness, this layering offers a projection of the human activity occurring in the space and a view through the entire volume. Within this system there are a number of openings where the panel system is hinged to operate as doors

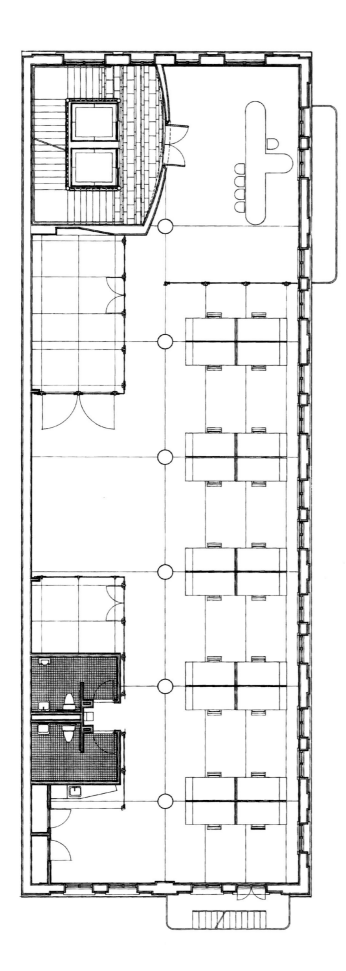

or movable door panels. The 15-foot-tall aluminum vertical support elements modulate the scale of the open space in addition to the rhythm of the connective elements that articulate the joinery of materials at a tactile scale. The entirety of assembled pieces were fabricated from stock aluminum that were bolted together and in form reflect the process of their manufacturing through the expression of cuts and drill holes. The furnishings were designed to complement the wall system and were fabricated of welded steel, metal laminated plywood, and metallic vinyl coverings for the barstools.

The walls, made from Plexiglas clipped together with aluminum squares, are frosted, though the Plexiglas at eye level is clear blue. The milky transparency provides an ethereal quality to the space that reflects the company's otherworldly business ideals—the company Web site boasts topics such as passion, reality, and freedom as well as a range of business ideas and models. Custom workstations, designed in collaboration with ATTIK's staff, are made of galvanized steel desks and chairs as well as more Plexiglas and were fabricated in Mexico under direct Rose's supervision. Like many young, high-tech firms, ATTIK incorporated iMACS into the design scheme, emphasizing a sleek, Modernist, and Minimalist experience.

This interior landscape of transparent and opaque walls is sited within the industrial aesthetic of galvanized windows and exposed brick of the turn-of-the-century building. The lightness of the material pallet allows the floor, walls, and ceiling of the space to extend beyond the foreground toward a sense of ambiguity.

◇ Rose designed the 4,000-square-foot office of ATTIK in collaboration with company CEO Will Travis.

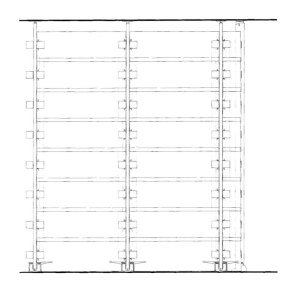

⊗ Rose custom developed Plexiglas
and aluminum anodized walls that
have wingbolts and adjustable
vertical parts so they are flexible
and can easily be moved for
future growth plans.

⊗ Above and Bottom, Right: The
⊘ drawings shown here are preliminary development sketches of
the walls.

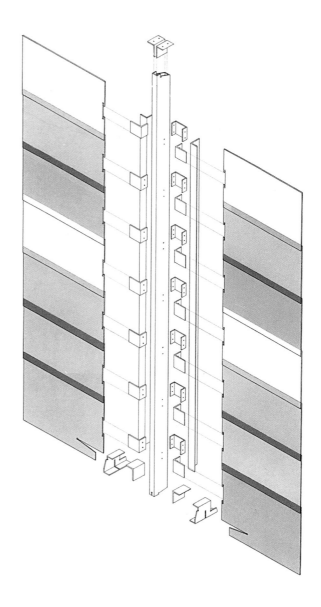

Left, Right, and Bottom: Custom workstations, designed in collaboration with ATTIK's staff, are made of galvanized steel desks and chairs as well as more Plexiglas.

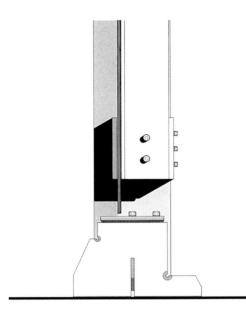

When the surreal productions of the **Axis Theatre Company,** an experimental ensemble that writes, produces, and performs original high-tech multimedia works, **needed a new venue, the company, and in particular**

⊘ With a clinical, laboratory-like feeling, the lower lobby is lined with glass cabinets that hold props and other artifacts. Back-lit images, such as the one seen on the door to the private office, can also be presented.

⊘ Stairs take visitors from the ground-level foyer to the lower lobby and theater. Messana O'Rorke chose a palette of materials that includes stainless steel, concrete, glass, and high-tech electronic media.

executive producer Jeffrey Resnick, asked Messana O'Rorke Architects to renovate the Greenwich Village space. Principals Brian Messana and Toby O'Rorke met with Resnick to discuss the upcoming project and the creative threesome collaborated on the design scheme. When Messana and O'Rorke finally took a look at the dilapidated basement space and the limited budget, they announced that they could translate the client's wishes into three-dimensional reality.

The 4,200-square-foot (390-square-meter) space, located at One Sheridan Square, has a rich theatrical history. First, it was home to the Café Society, New York's first racially integrated downtown club and the stage for Billie Holiday, Lena Horne, and Zero Mostel in the 1930s and 1940s. In the 1960s, the space became Sanctuary, a venue for Jimi Hendrix and other like-minded rock-and-roll musicians. Later, it housed Charles Ludlam's Ridiculous Theater Company until they vacated in 1994. With such a dramatic background and a charismatic current tenant, the space needed to make a comparable design statement.

The space started out as a complete wreck, with exposed pipes and conduits running everywhere, things falling apart, and a sewage system that constantly flooded with heavy rainfall. The architects immediately cleared the way and relocated gas pipes, sprinkler mains, soil pipes, and electrical conduits to bring the building systems to order. Then, the interior was completely gutted.

Once the space was clear, Messana O'Rorke created three distinct areas: a ground-level foyer, lower lobby, and theater. To begin, the foyer includes a sound system and a large, billboard-like sign that relates ever-changing information about the current production. Messana O'Rorke chose a palette of materials that includes stainless steel, concrete, glass, and high-tech electronic media. An LED sign hangs over the entrance to the theater, providing information that can be posted and altered as required.

Visitors descend into a lower lobby that has a clinical, laboratory-like feeling, lined with glass cabinets that hold props and other artifacts; these vitrines can also be used as light boxes for translucent images, similar to an X-ray viewing machine, as well as surface to affix supergraphics that present a continuous mural. A large central seating area, made of ebonized wood, provides a sleek design statement.

Architecturally, the theater is a simple plan; technologically, it is full and well equipped. The architects designed an intimate viewing arrangement with ninety-nine seats in a tiered semicircle around the stage. Even utilitarian spaces such as the dressing room were completely transformed into fully-functioning working areas. New stage flooring (a suspended plywood platform finished in continuous sheet vinyl), a soundproof control booth, and state-of-the-art sound (in collaboration with Steve Fontain), lighting (provided by David Zeffren), and projection systems (from Scharff Weisberg) round out the space. Additional backstage space was taken from the rear basement to ensure that the new theater is as functional as it is fresh.

Even utilitarian spaces such as the dressing room were completely transformed into fully-functioning working spaces.

⊗ The architects designed an intimate viewing arrangement with ninety-nine seats in a tiered semicircle around the stage.

The Danish company **Bang & Olufsen, a worldwide leader in audio/visual technology,** was founded in 1925. The company's factory was **destroyed during World War II** and a new one built in 1946.

To avoid conflict with the town's existing skyline, the Bang & Olufsen's building's highest point is no more than the church or town buildings' general height.

Since then, a number of additions have created a continuous band running south between the town of Struer and the Veno Bay to the east. The property between the factory and the bay belongs to the company and was the obvious choice for the architect Jans Søndergaard and KHRAS, who were commissioned to design the new headquarters.

Company management gave the architects full creative license to design the building from concept to detail. The sole request: they did not want a showroom but a building that expressed the Bang & Olufsen identity—simple, elegant, and innovative. At the same time, the building had to be unpretentious and built within a set budget. To meet this monetary goal, KHRAS designed all components and furniture (in collaboration with Fritz Hansen) as well as lighting.

Referred to as "the farm," due to the traditional Danish farm layout that inspired the design, the new site has a courtyard that forms an enclosed space and visual contact between all of the office functions and production. In respect to the older buildings, the new ones try to obtain a "quiet and almost weightless expression through transparency in the big, calm façades where materials are recognizable from the relation between building and landscape as seen in the visually subdued main entrance," says Søndergaard. Thus, access to the building is placed towards the open, untouched surrounding fields. Also, to avoid a conflict with the town's existing skyline, the building's highest point is no more than the church tower or town buildings' general height.

From the formal entrance and centrally-placed lobby with classic Danish designed chairs from Poul Kjærholm, visitors are introduced to the entire building complex. In contrast to the "calm" exterior, the interior forms a dynamic contrast to all functions and spaces. The layout of the public and common facilities as well as the circulation areas is along the open façades. This helps facilitate communication and visibility between employees. In spite of the simple geometry of the building volumes, their combination and juxtaposition creates spatial variations and complexity in relation to the landscape. This spatial variation is enforced by the choice in materials. The combination of glass, plaster, and brickwork creates a varied, yet highly controlled view towards both landscape and production facilities. Icelandic basalt, sand-blown glass, and the in-situ cast-concrete surfaces, together with the light wooden floors in the circulation areas, mediates a break in the open-plan layout of the building. So, a change of material, such as walking from a wooden floor to glass or along a closed façade to an open one, substitutes for traditional division of spaces created by doors or walls.

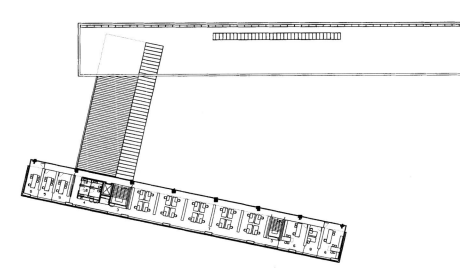

⊘ Icelandic basalt, sand-blown glass, and the in-situ cast-concrete surfaces, together with the light wooden floors in the circulation areas, mediates a break in the open-plan layout of the building.

⊘ The U-shaped plan consists of a northern wing, a connecting structure, and an office wing.

The U-shaped plan consists of a northern wing, a connecting structure, and the raised office wing. The northern wing (which includes the foyer, auditorium, meeting rooms, and dining area) faces toward the courtyard; the connecting building (which houses the marketing department and showroom) determines the width of the courtyard; and, with its modest height and closed character, the office wing acts as an independent building, built with a system of grid-like steel columns and beams that seems to float above the ground.

On all floors of the office wing, there are open workstations separated by custom-designed shelving walls. From the top of these units, light is projected on the ceiling, eliminating the need of individual fixtures on the desks. Small window slots in the south façade and a continuous glass façade on the north side control and filter daylight. At both ends of the space, office groups are separated by the same shelving units. At the east end are the executive offices; the west, management.

In the cast-concrete northern wing, the dining facility is furnished with identical rows of custom-designed long, black tables, providing an austere impression. Daylight comes through the south-facing windowed wall as well as skylights above. Also in the space are the subterranean auditorium, enclosed with glass walls, and meeting rooms off the upper corridor. A rough plate-glass staircase serves as a wind tower for the ventilation system, creating a low-pressure area.

Starting with a rural site and an ambitious, high-tech corporate client, Søndergaard created a headquarters with cool abstraction and graceful style that seems to float in mid air. The space is sensitive to both its history and current landscape and plays on traditional architecture as well as creating new ideas. Such a grand outcome should not go by unnoticed by rivals.

⊗ In the cast-concrete northern wing, the dining facility is furnished with identical rows of custom-designed long, black tables, providing an austere impression.

⊗ A rough plate-glass staircase serves as a wind tower for the ventilation system, creating a low-pressure area.

The office wing acts as an independent building, built with a system of grid-like steel columns and beams that seems to float above the ground.

As a fast-growing new division of an established company **with a highly visible reputation,** **barnesandnoble**.com needed new offices and computer facilities

to address current demands and allow for continual adaptation while providing a distinct identity for the newly created online division. Located in a former Port Authority building in New York's Chelsea district, the 65,000-square-foot (6,039-square-meter) office houses a staff of two hundred employees, including executives, business development staffers, and editors as well as space for financial, marketing, network, and production services, programming functions, meeting rooms, and employee amenities, such as a dining area furnished with classic Emeco chairs from ICF. Also included in the plan was a small office to house M&CO, the graphic design company led by Tibor Kalman, who had worked for the company over many years. The project's design director, Ross Anderson of Anderson Architects, describes the overall planning approach as a "loose-fit" to allow the office to be flexible in function and dynamic in use. A simple palette of materials was used, including exposed and painted concrete, raw and blackened steel, stainless-steel mesh, raw aluminum, plywood, translucent acrylic, plastic laminate, and marmoleum.

Organizing the facility, down to the lighting, wiring, and HVAC systems, was a challenge; integrating all of the workstation needs, open space, and service systems tested Anderson's design nerves as well as associate M.J. Sagan and project architect Todd Stodolski. A certain degree of hierarchy was required throughout the different workspaces, but the separation of levels within the hierarchy was to be minimal. As a result, three types of offices were created: perimeter offices for the executive level, strips of freestanding but enclosed

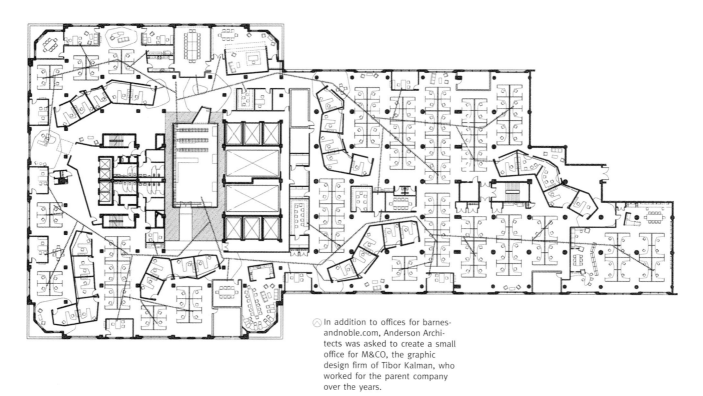

In addition to offices for barnesandnoble.com, Anderson Architects was asked to create a small office for M&CO, the graphic design firm of Tibor Kalman, who worked for the parent company over the years.

offices called "worms" for management level, and open workstations for all others. The design team worked with Unifor to create systems furniture and Office Specialty for filing needs. Also, they allotted generous space between the specific elements for unprogrammed, informal interaction. Area rugs, used as pools of color, are scattered throughout and highlight the open-area gathering spaces within the field of offices and workstations. Eames chairs are seen throughout the reception and unprogrammed spaces.

Within the hierarchy of spaces, several specific elements are distinguished. The entry, reception area, network operations center (NOC), and the high-tech conference room each hold a higher rank, informing the entry sequence and helping to orient the visitor. Visible directly from the elevator, a metal screen garage door hovers inside the entry, offering protection as the visitor arrives. Intense spotlights and custom ceiling-mounted light fixtures called Pringles further define these areas.

Perimeter offices alternate with open bays to preserve views to New Jersey and upper and lower Manhattan. Looking through the oversized windows, boldly painted "worm" offices slither between existing structural columns, marking different departments. "The cityscape and Hudson River views become wallpaper wrapping the space," says Anderson. "Workstations become the field. A forest of dark-painted concrete columns integrate the horizontal layers."

As visitors pass through the first of six "worm" constructions, an open area (referred to as "the clearing") is bordered by the conference room to the south and NOC to the north, beyond which lies a full-floor of offices. Custom "lily pad" rugs add color and rhythm to the floor. The NOC, the electronic innards of barnesandnoble.com, and sometimes referred to as "Oz," floats within the floor's former loading dock, where trucks once picked up and delivered cargo. The NOC can be seen through a galvanized metal viewport known around the offices as "the snout." The conference room includes a media cabinet and custom-designed conference table that is wired for multimedia presentations, videoconferencing, and laptops.

Anderson worked with certain constraints to create an organized office space. Three major requirements had to be acknowledged during the design phase: lighting, wiring, and ventilation. All three elements were critical to the new media venture and Web design in general. In response, the ceiling plane throughout the site is occupied by a "shifting plaid" of systems, says Anderson, that reaches down four-and-a-half vertical feet (1.4 meters) and includes linear fluorescent strip uplights, exposed cable trays and ductwork, electrical racks, and acoustical treatments designed with the help of acoustical and technological consulting from Shen Milsom & Wilke.

For ample security, the custom-designed reception desk is visible from the elevator lobby through a metal garage door.

Working with a minimal budget, limited schedule, multiple existing structural grids, a complex HVAC system, intense electrical and network cabling requirements, and the need for a state-of-the-art network operations center, Anderson Architects rose to the challenge and created a commercial/industrial site that can accommodate website offices. In addition, Anderson can't seem to get Chet Baker's jazz tune "Let's Get Lost" out of his mind when walking through the facility—the plan's scope and size is a bit daunting. However, Anderson likens the experience to surfing the Web; a most appropriate analogy.

The snout provides a sneak peak into the NOC, which is heavily guarded behind chain-link fencing.

Perimeter offices and open workstations have great views and take advantage of natural daylight.

The high-tech conference room includes a custom-designed table that is wired for multi-media presentations.

Bates, an international advertising agency,

retained STUDIOS to design all seven floors of their **new United States headquarters in New York.**

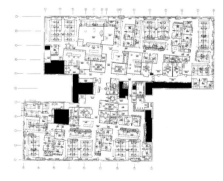

Having already undergone a series of organizational changes, the agency sought to maximize its real estate usage from a cost as well as humanistic perspective. STUDIOS' approach included an initial occupancy analysis, which concluded with the agency's decision to move from the historic Chrysler Building to 498 7th Avenue, a site in what was once primarily New York's garment district. The decision to relocate would reduce real estate costs, but would also allow the agency the opportunity to create an environment tailored specifically to their client's needs.

The challenge for STUDIOS was to design a space that would support the creative nature of advertising. Specifically, Bates sought to improve work processes by encouraging interaction among staff, enabling communication, and providing a "home" where work could occur in a wide range of settings. The result is a flexible, dynamic environment that will support Bates through future organizational and technical changes. The presentation area on the second floor features automatic sliding doors that open to connect distinct rooms into one large meeting area. This flexible arrangement allows the client presentations to be tailored—small intimate groups or large formal gatherings can be accommodated in the same zone.

A reception area greets visitors and a central, glass-enclosed stair is flanked by a coffee bar on each of Bates' seven floors and connects staff visually and spatially, providing a framework for communication and interaction. At any given time, graphic designers, human resources personnel, media buyers, and account executives travel the stair en route to the cafeteria, the presentation area, or central resources.

⊘ The international advertising agency Bates retained STUDIOS to design all seven floors of their New York headquarters at 498 7th Avenue, a site in what was once primarily New York's garment district.

To complement a primarily open floor plan, STUDIOS designed a wide array of meeting and private spaces. Individual workstations are part of larger neighborhoods, where a variety of meeting rooms and amenities are accessible to support a range of needs and functions. Central to any neighborhood are equipment hubs, small quiet rooms, basic conference rooms, and project rooms.

In addition to designing the space, STUDIOS provided transition services aimed at helping the agency adopt shifts in work processes. STUDIOS' staff, along with key individuals at Bates, developed long-term strategies and implemented programs that communicated changes and progress in the design to staff.

The presentation area on the second floor features automatic sliding doors that open to connect distinct rooms into one large meeting area.

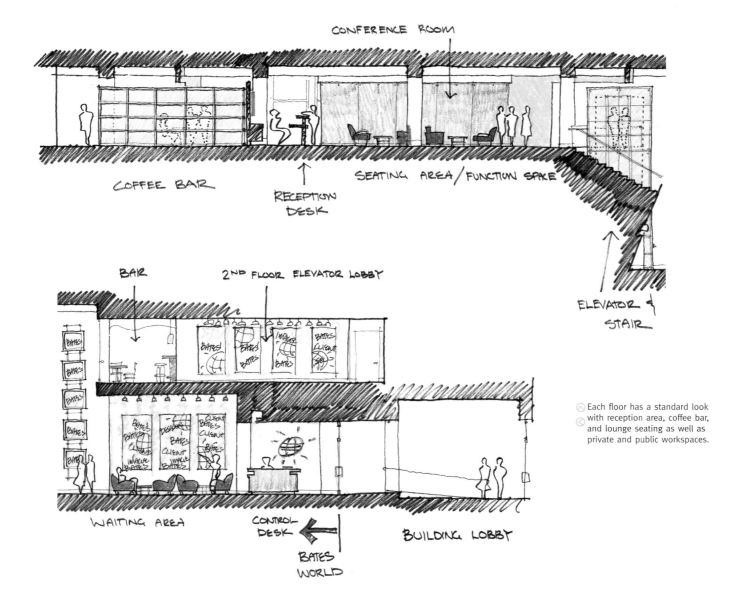

CONFERENCE ROOM

COFFEE BAR

RECEPTION DESK

SEATING AREA / FUNCTION SPACE

ELEVATOR & STAIR

BAR

2ND FLOOR ELEVATOR LOBBY

WAITING AREA

CONTROL DESK

BATES WORLD

BUILDING LOBBY

Each floor has a standard look with reception area, coffee bar, and lounge seating as well as private and public workspaces.

A reception area greets visitors; a display wall provides company information for both employees and clients.

Individual workstations are part of larger neighborhoods, where a variety of meeting rooms and amenities are accessible to support a range of needs and functions.

⊗ Central to any neighborhood are
⊗ equipment hubs, small quiet
rooms, basic conference rooms,
and project rooms.

⊗ The stair is used by all personnel
to access the cafeteria, presentation area, and central resources.

Blue **Hypermedia,** a leading on-line design and consulting firm specializing in **creating websites** for **emerging and established branded products,** works closely with clients, such as

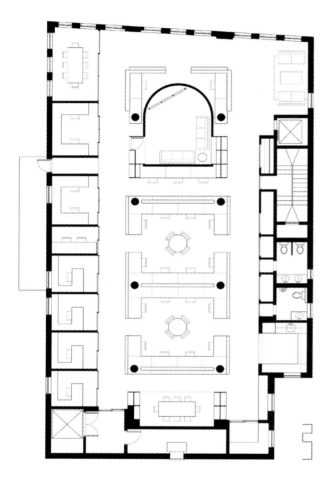

Blue Hypermedia worked with the New York firm Specht Harpman to create a "cool" but not self-important identity for their company.

Mastercard, MTV Interactive, Insignia/ESG, Douglas Elliman, Kahlua, Pepsi, and Mars Company. The company helps clients target e-commerce opportunities and creates on-line identities for their products, offering a comprehensive package of business development, design, and technical consulting services.

The New York-based firm Specht Harpman, with a team led by project designers Scott Specht and Louise Harpman and project director Amy Lopez-Cepero, who share a similar "soup-to-nuts" strategy when taking on new projects, worked closely with the three partners at Blue Hypermedia to envision a productive, yet relaxed environment for their company. Blue Hypermedia asked the architects to create a "cool," but not self-important identity for their company. Within the large, open-plan room (nicknamed the "War Room"), Specht Harpman developed a system of custom desks, dividers, data storage units, and lighting that allows for both individual workstations and distinct teams. A row of offices flanks the long wall of the loft, at once screening the harsh southern light and also allowing for a degree of enclosure for private meetings.

For this project, Specht Harpman was able to pursue its interest in new materials and fabrication assemblies. As an example, the wall of offices is a custom steel assembly with integral door frames and sliding door hardware; the frames hold hex-cell plastic panels, which are viewed very differently when seen in natural and incandescent lighting. This same industrial plastic is used for the partitions on the "War Room," allowing for some visual screening while offering a seductive play of light across the material.

The office features a large enclosed screening room, two open-plan teamwork areas, private offices, reception, pantry, lounge, and conference room.

Within the large, open-plan room (the "War Room"), Specht Harpman developed a system of custom desks, dividers, data storage units, and lighting that allows for both individual work-stations and distinct teams.

⊗ The "War Room" has space
⊘ for both individual and team
workstations.

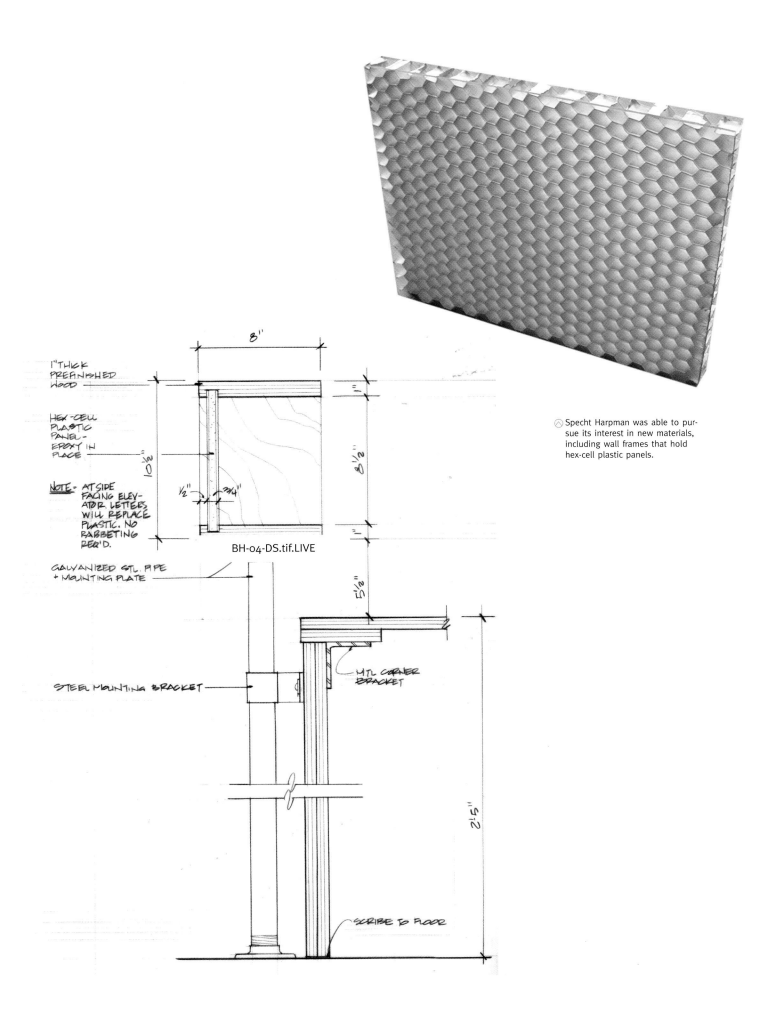

8"

1" THICK
PREFINISHED
WOOD

HEX-CELL
PLASTIC
PANEL-
EPOXY IN
PLACE

10 1/2"

1"

8 1/2"

1/2"   3/4"

NOTE: AT SIDE
FACING ELEV-
ATOR. LETTERS
WILL REPLACE
PLASTIC. NO
RABBETING
REQ'D.

1"

BH-04-DS.tif.LIVE

⬡ Specht Harpman was able to pursue its interest in new materials,
including wall frames that hold
hex-cell plastic panels.

GALVANIZED STL. PIPE
+ MOUNTING PLATE

5 1/2"

STEEL MOUNTING BRACKET

MTL CORNER
BRACKET

2'5"

SCRIBE TO FLOOR

CarsDirect.Com is an on-line car buying service **whose success is built on speed and simplicity**—the company moves product quickly; it moves goods to market quickly;

⊘ Gensler was awarded the CarsDirect.Com project, an interactive, flexible, 43,000-square-foot (3,995-square-meter) contiguous space on a single floor in a warehouse-style building.

⊘ To accommodate the client's high-tech needs, the Gensler design team created a server room that is built into the space and integrates the ceiling's truss system.

its consumers move quickly and simply through the website; and dealerships are attracted by its efficiency and straightforwardness. CarsDirect.Com held a competition that called for a fast-track design solution. The three-day event resulted in Gensler's selection for their design of an interactive, flexible, 43,000-square-foot (3,995-square-meter) contiguous space on a single floor in a warehouse-style building. The client had two primary goals in developing its new space: to create a space that would imply market permanence and business competence and to develop a facility that conveyed an energetic corporate culture to employees and recruits. The company had also experienced a tremendous growth spurt. When Gensler had first landed the contract, the company employed fifty people; at the onset of the program, two hundred twenty; two hundred fifty people at the time the design was finished; and outgrew two hundred fifty seats by the time of occupancy.

With a condensed schedule (one hundred twenty days total to design and build) and a tight budget, Gensler implemented its design in a phased process, choosing readily available, contractor-friendly materials and working closely with all the consultants and the client to achieve the overall design goals. Phase one included a one-hundred-fifty-seat call center that took sixty days to build from design to occupancy. Phase two (for the remainder of the space) took eighty days from design to build to occupancy. The design team, including director Gene Watanabe, designer Terence Young, technical architect Will Chung, and project manager Bill Gilliland, used 3-D design tools to communicate more efficiently with consultants and help solve issues relating to the intersection of the building structure and its impact on HVAC, lighting, and technology interface. Other architectural features include ceiling space with an open truss system integrated with building systems, open conference areas, a high-tech server room, a metal-clad formal boardroom

with full Web-based communications and presentation audio/video capability, large-screen Web-connected projection television to monitor a website in real time.

The open warehouse allowed for a grand reception/entryway as well as a large number of open, customized workstations. Customization was achieved inexpensively by working closely with furniture manufacturers who used sustainable, recycled, available materials. The workstations were strategically situated around a data spine that feeds power/lighting walls. Teaming areas were incorporated near the art and marketing departments.

In the ever-changing, fast-paced dot-com world, CarsDirect.Com wanted a corporate space that would convey stability, business savvy, and dynamic energy, while accommodating rapid growth and development. Gensler provided an efficient, straightforward design that integrated high-tech with high style.

The metal-clad formal boardroom has full Web-based communications and presentation capabilities.

CarsDirect.Com's new offices are
housed in an open warehouse
that allowed for a grand reception and an entryway with a
ceiling of open trusses.

The warehouse allowed for a large number of open, customized workstations that utilized sustainable, recycled, available materials. The workstations were strategically situated around a data spine that feeds power/lighting walls.

Los Angeles and the Hollywood scene provides a haven for digital effects and computer animation companies like Click3XLA; especially in Santa Monica's Bergamot Station arts complex,

a collection of forty-five industrial buildings converted into art galleries and spaces for art-related tenants, where the company's new production office stands. Housed in a 9,000-square-foot (836-square-meter) portion of a 30,000-square-foot (2,787-square-meter) industrial building (once used to manufacture residential water heaters), the space was renovated by Los Angeles architects Pugh & Scarpa and is in keeping with the client's main request: move into a completed space in less than sixteen weeks from the beginning of the design process.

In order to meet this demand, client, contractor, and architect vowed to collaborate with unprecedented synergism. The architects also had to be creative in their conceptual thinking and in choreographing the design and construction process. The program was strategically divided into distinct areas that could be developed in phases with the construction schedule. Each programmatic element was explored in depth and developed in detail, presented to the client, and then dimensioned and issued to the contractor for construction. Design decisions were made in close association with the contractor and various fabricators whose expertise was fundamental to the project. Construction began during the first fourteen days of design and city permits were issued by the beginning of the third week. All project drawings that were generated served as both client presentation and construction document. To facilitate the process, all drawings were either computer generated or drawn freehand on vellum. The immediacy of working in this "one take" or "live broadcast" context resulted in architecture that, in essence, evolved as a drawing at full scale.

The plan includes Inferno rooms, spaces dedicated to creating visual effects and computer animation for television commercials and shows and large-format movies. Also included in the program are several other computer animation studios, avid rooms, CGI suites, open production space, conference rooms, executive offices, and a machine room housing sophisticated visual effects computers.

When the garage door is up, the lounge area of Click3XLA's space can be used for parties.

A conceptual rendering from the architects, viewing the entire project.

Click3XLA maintains a spatial community and sensation of vastness characteristic of the industrial warehouse buildings at Bergamot Station. Light reaches into the space via a generous wall of windows at the entry. Attention was paid to maintaining and constructing unbroken visual corridors that extend the entire length of the space. A simply finished concrete slab creates a continuous monochromatic ground surface that helps preserve and emphasize this spatial flow. Simultaneously, the architecture creates opportunities for more intimate, isolated moments.

The freestanding, irregularly shaped Inferno unit, where Click's computer wizards work their magic, divides the interior into two discrete but interconnected areas, each anchored by a lounge area in order to keep clients selling similar products away from each other, keeping Coca-Cola and Pepsi free to talk openly about projects, says principal Lawrence Scarpa. The northern area serves as the main entrance. When open, the entry has a large 16 ft. x 16 ft. (4.9 m x 4.9 m) garage door that directly links up with the public space of the Bergamot Station Arts Complex. This space, frequently used for client parties, says the architects, acts as a more formal covered porch. At the south end, the public space features a galley kitchen and informal lounge as well as a freestanding, cylindrical conference room. Natural light filters in through skylights, the glazed façade, and the garage door. A mezzanine level is occupied by the worker bees.

The more specific and specialized programmatic elements of Click3XLA (Inferno rooms, computer animation studios, etc.) are asymmetrically placed along the western edge of the corridor. The animate, opaque, and sculpturally expressive forms of these freestanding spaces are countered by a simply expressed linear bar housing executive suites along the perimeter wall. The twelve-foot-high (3.7-meter) metal stud walls that define the executive bar features a corrugated translucent fiberglass skin, which allows light to filter in from the exterior. A play on the sanctity of public and private space is evident in the materials chosen to articulate the various areas. For example, the most private and individual office cells are screened behind a translucent and filmy skin while the more public gathering rooms are hidden behind opaque surfaces.

According to Pugh & Scarpa, the architecture of Click3XLA is "intended to confront the user. Bold, almost primitive sculptural forms are intentionally large and expressive. The intent is to challenge and stimulate." They continue: "A movement between intimate enclosed space and open exposed space reflects a pattern inherent in all human beings as we navigate the daily boundary between the privacy of our own thoughts and feelings and the publicness of our everyday lives."

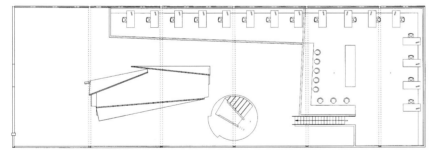

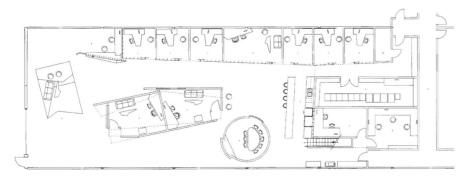

Top: Separate effects and editing suites are architecturally distinctive from the rest of the space.

Middle: Floor plan of the conference room and production areas that accommodate editing needs as well as client interaction with some privacy.

Bottom: A floor plan of the entire facility, including the reception, offices, production, and kitchen areas.

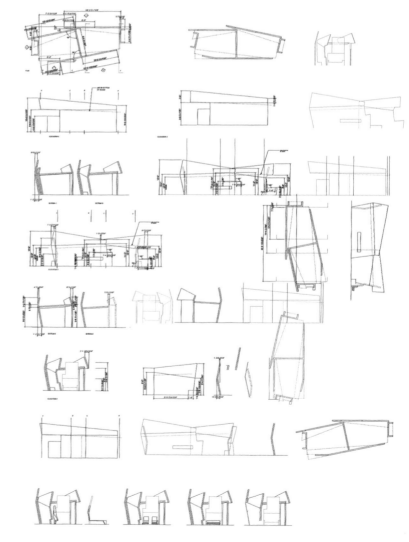

Shown here is the freestanding Inferno room, reception, and lounge areas. Corrugated fiber-glass panels are fastened to exposed galvanized metal studs that enclose executive offices.

Bottom Left: Around the office, the conference room is referred to as "bean dip and tortillas" for its unusual top and cylindrical girth.

Bottom Right: This series of Inferno elevations was the beginning of what would eventually become the final design scheme of the editing suite.

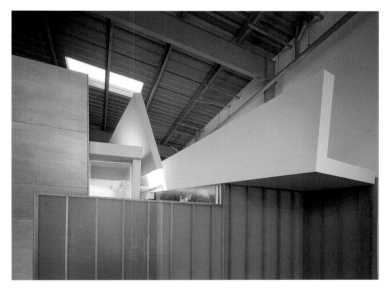

⊗ Bold, primitive sculptural forms
⊗ are intentionally large and
expressive to create an intense
visual impact.

⊗ Pugh & Scarpa took advantage
of the natural light with well-
placed skylights and a large front
window wall.

Clickthings, a multinational software development company, was launched in the **fall of** 1999. As a member of the **New York City Investment Fund,**

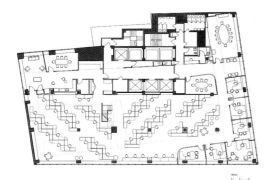

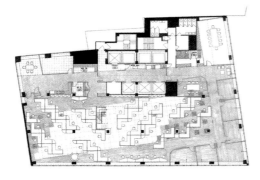

the company chose to locate their new offices in New York City and specifically at 110 Wall Street so they could closely interact. The project consists of the complete design and renovation of the ninth floor and partial renovation of the tenth floor totaling 20,000 square feet (1,858 square meters). As with all their corporate clients, the New York-based architectural and design firm Fox & Fowle got involved in this project with the development of a program of requirements. However, it soon became clear early in the process that the design of the space plan was going to help mold the branding of Clickthings' corporate identity. Clickthings requested offices that would project their forward thinking, modern attitude, while at the same time suggest a stable presence to their clients and investors.

The design team at Fox & Fowle, including project director Rodney VenJohn, project designer/architect Douglass Alligood, project co-designer Michael Stark, and project team Erica Joltin, Danielle Hricay, Bess Long, and Robert Lanni, established two zones within the space. The first zone is the public face including a reception area with interactive media walls. The reception area is situated on axis with the elevators and leads to large perimeter windows with sweeping views of the South Street Seaport and East River. Although Clickthings installed a central stairwell antenna, which allows wireless Internet and network access, a supplemental antenna was installed in the large conference room making this a true state-of-the-art teleconferencing center. This room contains computer-equipped audio/visual presentation capabilities and is completed with flexible furniture so that individual presentations or office-wide meetings can happen here. Materials selected for this front area include embossed vinyl flooring, maple veneer panels, translucent extruded PVC panels, and galvanized metal deck. A continuous boldly painted wall that says Clickthings in orange slices through these spaces and unifies these elements.

⊗ Top: Reception, situated on axis with the elevators, leads to large perimeter windows with views of the South Street Seaport and East River.

⊗ The conference room, located in the more public zone, has high-tech audio/visual presentation capabilities and flexible furniture so that individual presentations or office-wide meetings can happen here.

⊗ The designers presented a full materials palette that included embossed vinyl flooring, maple veneer panels, translucent extruded PVC panels, and galvanized metal deck.

The second zone consists of open office workstations, private offices, informal meeting areas, and a multipurpose playroom. The back support area received the same dynamic treatment of over-lapping geometries that accentuate the asymmetrical layout of the building. Much effort was placed on representing the egalitarian atmosphere of the company. Private offices are kept to a minimum. The open office incorporates nonlinear circulation patterns, informal work areas, and visibility to perimeter windows. The ceiling is left high and open and is outlined by floating planes of hung acoustical tile. Ductwork and cable trays are exposed as feature elements. They are placed, along with linear uplights on a consistent, parallel forty-five-degree angle and reinforce the primary and secondary circulation paths on the floor.

Privacy walls were necessary for financial officers and legal council but were installed in a "nuts-and-bolts" fashion. Translucent extruded PVC panels and galvanized metal deck are used in place of the more traditional sheetrock and glass and are simply screwed to metal studs. By seeing conduit and cable running through the PVC panels, Fox & Fowle expresses and celebrates the methods by which we all receive our information.

A new, lightweight, freestanding panel system (called Passage by Herman Miller) is used in open areas. The typical workstation for Web designers and strategists is a 7 ft. x 7 ft. (2.1 m x 2.1 m) L-shaped module, which, when arranged in continuous rows, provides uninterrupted surface for shared dialogue and shared equipment. The system's thin panels are translucent, curved, or minimized in height allowing continuous sight lines throughout the space. Impromptu meetings and conversation nooks are incorporated into the voids that are created within the systems furniture clusters. These nooks are outfitted with traditional tables and chairs, comfortable lounge seating, and even low, egg-shaped stools where staff members can perch during quick wireless Internet jaunts. Furniture used in perimeter offices is components from the same panel system and is used sparingly and efficiently.

The multipurpose room in the rear is outfitted with a full kitchen, game tables, televisions, and lounge furniture. Inexpensive materials such as plastic laminate and vinyl tile were used here, but by mixing multiple patterns and colors together, the effect is both playful and practical.

The designers' vision for the space exceeded the client's goals for the project. The space not only fosters the creativity needed to allow Clickthings to continue to be a success, but also helps create the brand image to separate itself from the competition and attract top new talent.

Top: The original sketches for the display gallery includes technical information about certain materials and products that are used to exhibit industry information.

Bottom: The overall floor plan of the executive theater space offers a complete view of the 3,250-square-foot (292.5-square-meters) facility, showing the plan of the display gallery outside the theater, as well as other office space.

For certain employees, privacy walls were necessary. However, they were installed in a "nuts-and-bolts" fashion with translucent extruded PVC panels and galvanized metal deck.

The typical workstation is an L-shaped module that provides uninterrupted surface for shared dialogue and equipment. The system's thin panels are translucent, curved, or minimized in height allowing continuous sight lines throughout the space.

In 1996, when Condé Nast announced that it would be consolidating its media empire under one roof, approximately 760,000 square feet of space in **Manhattan's 4 Times Square building on Broadway** between 42nd and 43rd Streets,

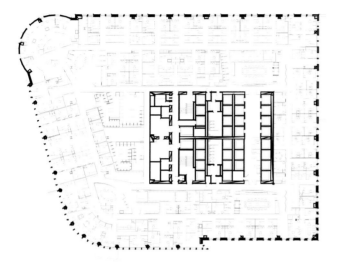

Condé Nast's new offices include approximately 760,000 square feet of space in Manhattan's 4 Times Square building on Broadway between 42nd and 43rd Streets. The New York-based firm Mancini Duffy was retained to provide complete interior planning, design, and architectural services.

Mancini Duffy was retained to provide complete interior planning, design, and architectural services. Condé Nast occupies 18 floors of the new building, a $500 million, 48-story glass-and-granite structure designed by the New York architectural firm Fox & Fowle.

The building developer, The Durst Organization, was committed to the use of environmentally sensitive materials and requested that tenants of the building conform to the green design guidelines. In keeping with this commitment to the environment, Mancini Duffy conducted extensive research for all interior systems and materials, examining such aspects as life cycle processes, recyclable materials content, sustainability of wood products, and manufacturers' environmental commitment.

Each floor houses two magazines, with the exception of *Vogue, Vanity Fair,* and *The New Yorker,* and each floor has a similar footprint. Each floor has a shared reception area; behind the glass security doors is a branding wall with the resident magazine logo. An "art corridor," where company archives are displayed, slices past the branding wall and connects the office's outer walkways. A cantilevered relief, finished in encaustic rub, frames the art works.

Behind the branding wall stands a 750-square-foot, high-tech conference room with an ash-veneered, dark-stained table and a mohair-upholstered banquette along the wall for additional seating. The fabric-covered walls and carpet are either gray or beige. A 350-square-foot meeting space with a glass wall at the far end of the art corridor is reserved for editorial use.

The majority of private offices are placed on the interior and open landscape workstations are used throughout a majority of the space, enabling employees to benefit from the greatest amount of daylight. Indirect and task lighting provide maximum flexibility and reduce electrical use. Art departments are along the western corners and have a curved window wall and natural light.

Smaller, interior meeting spaces, with glass walls, are used for formal and informal gatherings by editorial staff.

All workstations and interior office systems are from the Italian company Unifor and seating is from Girsberger; white laminate, a blue-gray aluminum, and wood veneer are the overall material choices. Executive suites were custom designed by either a team from Mancini Duffy or outside designers; each has a private washroom. Residential-style test kitchens were created for eight editors at *Gourmet* as well as two private dining rooms and an in-house photo studio.

Overall, the design is standardized but individual magazines customized their space at their respective elevator branding walls, and the primary corridor on each floor includes a display wall that each magazine can individualize at their discretion. Mancini Duffy's quiet and elegant design set the tone for the new corporate offices of Condé Nast.

Each art department runs along the southwestern corner and has a curved window wall for full access to natural daylight.

Most of Condé Nast's private offices are placed on the interior, with direct access to the open workstations. Some employees had their offices designed by Mancini Duffy, while others retained outside designers.

With due credit given to CEO Steven Golden, **Coolsavings.com,** a five-and-a-half-year-old **nationwide technology firm** specializing in **electronic coupon savings** via the Internet,

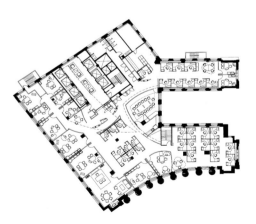

recently relocated their operations to a historical landmark building in downtown Chicago from a not-so-hip space near O'Hare airport. Now situated on the Chicago River at the corner of Michigan Avenue, the new offices, in a building originally designed by architect Alfred S. Alschuler in 1923, affords spectacular views of the skyline in all directions and is steps away from the city's shopping mecca. The building floor plate, character, and volume of space are also quite unique and the company wanted to work with a design firm to create an office with a similar dynamic within a distinctive setting.

Coolsavings.com hired the local firm Partners by Design and asked the team to preserve some of the old and add some high-tech flair. They also wanted to maintain a pool of talented employees, most of which come from Generation X; so the team could not create anything less than a thoroughly appealing work environment. Golden had leased more than 50,000 square feet (4,645 square meters) on the 8th, 18th, 19th, and 21st floors, plus common areas. Partners by Design had their work cut out for them.

The design team, including project architect, Ted Garnett, project director Jackie Ground, and project designer James Dolenc, initially responded by focusing on the synergies between the different work groups that make up Coolsavings.com and how these groups work together. They worked with the information services department and database groups and the consulting engineer to design and incorporate all systems requirements for the support of their business focus. In addition, Partners by Design's primary focuses were the provision of creative amenities such as recreational space to help encourage interaction and communication (specifically, a meeting room that converts into a basketball court), and the integration of open office teaming areas and small private conference facilities. As Coolsavings.com moved into an older office building, Partners by Design coordinated with the building landlord to help identify base building systems required to provide the necessary backbone for the client. Upgrades to the building were required for MEP and communication systems.

Partners by Design created 50,000 square feet of new office and recreation space for Coolsavings.com.

The point of entry on the 19th floor includes original marble lintels above the elevators, tile mosaics, and industrial room dividers. The main reception features theatrical-quality projected signage and a custom millwork reception desk with perforated metal screens, multi-level moveable glass transaction surfaces, and a built-in monitor. A brushed aluminum and corrugated translucent fiberglass tensile structure forms a backdrop for the desk and screens the reception area from the open office space beyond. A media tower with three LCD flat screens address visitors as they approach the reception desk, and features online video streaming, promotional videos, and website demos. Views from the reception area include the metallic-glass tiled curvilinear wall of the executive boardroom. Contemporary furniture and custom-designed rugs extend the reception space out into the refinished 1920s marble elevator lobby. After business hours, the lobby space is separated from the office and reception by a twelve-foot (3.7-meter) stainless-steel rolling overhead door. The basic color palette is gold and plum, Coolsavings.com corporate colors.

Partners by Design collaborated with Trendway Corp. to develop an innovative, open office furniture system based on Trendway's Contrada Raw, essentially a metal skeleton of the typical workstation, for two floors. The exposed structural and electrical elements of a standard workstation were used as design elements to express the support and infrastructure required by these technologically advanced users. Innovative and unusual materials, such as wire mesh and corrugated fiberglass, were integrated within the structural framework in order to create a unique solution. They added soft materials to absorb sound and avoid a noisy office—for example, file cabinets with cloth and cushions that double as seating for workstation guests. For two hundred fifty workstations, three designs were used: 3 ft. x 5 ft. (0.9 m x 1.5 m) hoteling stations for consultants and other temporary visitors; 6 ft. x 6 ft. (1.8 m x 1.8 m) administration assistants and accounting staff; and 6 ft. x 8 ft. (1.8 m x 2.4 m) for the development and product-support employees. Between the workstations, the designers provided space for teaming areas. Each floor has kitchenettes with Starbucks and there is even talk of Coolsavings.com hiring a hospitality manager to freshen the Sumatra and organize company events.

Today's market is competitive and retaining the most talented employees is critical to the success of a technology-based firm. With the notion of stock options rapidly fading, Partners by Design worked closely with the savvy dot.com client to offer an enticing environment to keep employees motivated and happy; and something with visual interest and pop and panache.

⊘ Creative amenities, such as recreational space to help encourage interaction (specifically, a meeting room that converts into a basketball court), was a top priority.

⊘ The designers included open office teaming areas and small private conference facilities in the design scheme.

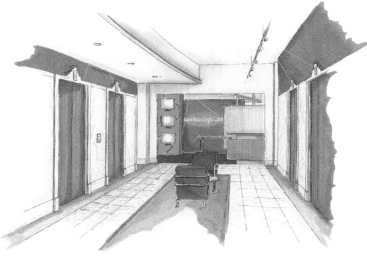

The main reception area features theatrical-quality projected signage and a custom millwork desk.

Each floor is equipped with kitchenettes and Starbucks coffee.

Partners by Design collaborated with Trendway Corp. to develop an innovative, open office furniture system based on a metal skeleton. Between the workstations, the designers provided space for teaming areas.

Bruce Goodman trained as an architect with Guillermo Garita in the early 1990s. Instead of pursuing his intended career, Goodman founded **Digital Pulp, an I-builder company** that specializes in e-commerce, brand strategy, corporate identity,

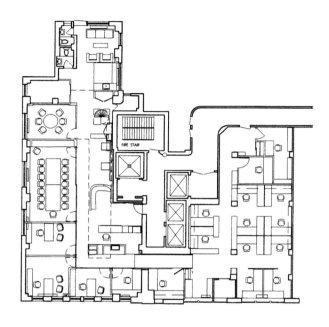

⊗ Datum/O developed a new plan for ninth floor that included 6,000 square feet (558 square meters) and connectivity to the tenth floor that incorporated 3,000 square feet (279 square meters).

and Web architecture with clients such as AltaVista and DoubleClick. When the company grew from ten people to sixty people in a quick year and a half, Goodman decided to take on more space and contacted Garita, who had founded his firm Datum/O in the meantime, to create new corporate offices. Principal in charge Guillermo Garita and design associate Julia Mock worked closely with Goodman to address some basic concerns. "The space needed to speak to what the company does," says Garita. "The generating premise was to create a spatial metaphor coherent to the founding roots of Digital Pulp, to establish an architectural language representational of their ideals." Garita continues, "Goodman needed to be presented with a convincing argument explaining the dynamics of Digital Pulp. We provided it."

Digital Pulp is divided into two areas: the digital, virtual work and hard copy work such as print ads and billboards. The company is based on exploring the joining of these two disciplines. Garita presented ideas about how the space could represent these two opposite ends through the use of materials including translucent, ephemeral resources as well as more tactile ones.

Of the three floors—the penthouse and two floors below—Datum/O developed a new plan for ninth floor that included 6,000 square feet (558 square meters) and connectivity to the tenth floor that incorporated 3,000 square feet (279 square meters). Upon entering the space, visitors are greeted by a reception and sitting area and then given a choice between two wings. Wing A includes the conference room, gallery, reception, and lounge, the more communal areas, while Wing B is dedicated to the creative department. An orange rubber tunnel connects the two areas. The joint of the two buildings, done by the landlord years ago, dictated the configuration. "It wasn't a very interesting transition so we glorified it and made it an appealing connection," says Garita.

⊗ The reception desk, in the communal space that includes the waiting area, is made of the same rubber/concrete material as the conference room table.

There are three key elements that yield a system of organization and a system of representation for the entire project. At the entry point, visitors are confronted by the first element, an amorphic, soft form sheathed with blue rubber that operates as the seating area. It rests on a hard seamless concrete continuous surface and also functions as the hinge point for the space. The second element is the orange tunnel, which exploits the transition of the two adjoining buildings as well as the connection of two very different programs. "It does not negate the connection but negotiates it, celebrates it," says Garita. The third component is a continuous line of fixed and operable translucent Plexiglas panels, uninterrupted from floor to ceiling defining the private and public areas. The custom made operable panels are hardwareless; they open and close with magnets.

Other secondary elements are a large sliding translucent wall that divides the conference room and the gallery. During large gatherings, the wall opens and gives way to the gallery. Display panels in the gallery rotate from the wall to collapse into tables. Because Goodman wanted a conference table large enough to accommodate eighteen to twenty people, Datum/O custom designed and built one

on site. The surface is made from the same concrete material used for the reception area, allowing for a strong visual and physical connection. A continuous folding steel plate that rises from the floor defines the reception desk; it is balanced with a translucent Plexiglas housing storage. The box is intervened by a smaller steel box that operates as a transaction top for incoming and outgoing packages.

The server room, once a hidden space that simply housed computer equipment, now becomes an architectural statement. The exposed room brings all of the gear outside; the unit is made of translucent Plexiglas and divides the lounge area from part of the creative department. With a flip of a few switches, the Plexiglas can even change colors and textures.

Digital Pulp wanted something different, a progressive space that represented new ideas. Since their founder is a trained architect, Datum/O found that employees were encouraged to participate in plan critiques and presentations. "They were very demanding about certain ideas," says Garita, "but that made for constant interesting interaction between architect and client."

At Digital Pulp, an orange rubber tunnel connects the public and private spaces.

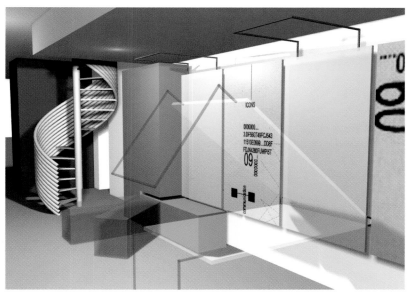

 Display panels in the gallery
rotate from the wall to collapse
into tables.

A continuous hive of Plexiglas
panels defines office areas.

Resolved to contain its scattered workforce, **DoubleClick,** a broker for advertising on the Web and one of the **fastest growing computer-based communications companies**

DoubleClick rented out the twelfth floor of a former warehouse, bringing the total square footage to 165,000.

in New York City's Silicon Alley, chose as their new headquarters a late-1960s building's sixteenth floor penthouse formerly taken over by an ice-skating rink. The venue is a converted light-industry warehouse on Manhattan's West 33rd Street. At 50,000 square feet (4,645 square meters), with "mezzanines" adding another 15,000 square feet (1,394 square meters), the space was not adequate. So DoubleClick rented out the twelfth floor, which soon brought the total to 165,000 square feet (15,329 square meters).

The Phillips Group, led by principal-in-charge Frederic Strauss and senior project designer Daniel Jacoby with the added help of Edgar Krois, Kevin Driscoll, Jane Yang, Jason Carney, Steve Gochman, Kevin Gold, Gabriel Sarmiento, Nelson Wong, and Donna Cuoco, designed the firm's new offices. Strauss and Jacoby started with the client's directives. The interior had to be forward-looking but not trendy; it had to make a statement about the company's status and have amenities to attract and keep the firm's eight hundred employees (95 percent of whom sit in open workstations). Finally, dynamics and flexibility had to be inherent attractions.

According to the designers, orderly organization of such a large-scale project tends to benefit from deployment of a theme, so the layout follows the pattern of a well-planned city. In typical new media form, the reception areas became gathering places, welcoming visitors but also providing a hangout for employees. However, allusions to boulevards and streets, civic landmarks, town squares, and a grand central park, the twelfth and sixteenth floors as well as two newly constructed "mezzanines," loosely comparable to two platforms linked by bridges and propped by columns matching those on lower floors, are the space's highlights. Each floor has a grand boulevard running its length, with special functions developed as unique architectural events, analogous to civil landmarks. This includes a park area at the center of the boulevard on the sixteenth floor, which includes seating and live Ficus trees. On the twelfth floor, the boulevard is defined by an open-cell suspended aluminum ceiling that widens as it progresses through the space. On both floors, blocks of enclosed offices defined the boundaries of different "neighborhoods" of workstation clusters. The neighborhood metaphor is further reinforced by local color coding of certain wall planes and accent fabrics on the workstations.

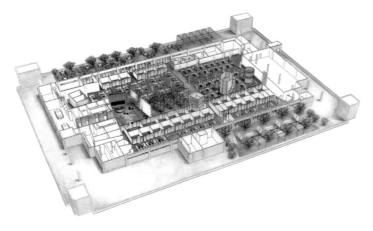

On the sixteenth floor, large openings in the upper flat open up sight lines to activities fourteen feet (4.3 meters) below. It is here, in this double-decker penthouse, that marketing, executive, customer service, and sales personnel occupy 6 ft. x 8 ft. (1.8 m x 2.4 m), 6 ft. x 6 ft. (1.8 m x 1.8 m), or 5 ft. x 5 ft. (1.5 m x 1.5 m) "lasagna noodle-shaped" workstations. At its highest point, as seen through the central opening in the added level, the ceiling rises to twenty-six feet (7.9 meters); at perimeters, the reach is just twelve feet (3.7 meters). Breaking up and optically loosening the stretch of workstations are vertically stacked pairs of metal-and-glass drums and wooden boxes, each twin-pack measuring twenty-four feet (7.3 meters) tall and collectively containing four meeting rooms. A similar effect of deregimentation is conveyed by the few enclosed offices positioned at slightly askew angles, by a tilted wall on each of the boxes, and by slightly protruding tops of other enclosures resembling, according to the spokesmen, baseball caps.

The reception area, a popular hang out, includes a custom desk, buffet, and soda dispensary. The stairs lead to the mezzanine.

The twelfth floor houses a 15,000-square-foot (1,394-square-meter) data center (the lifeline at DoubleClick's operations), programming, and engineering staff. Two large terraces facing east and west provide spectacular views of midtown Manhattan and the Hudson River and feature plug and play capability. An eatery gives employees a chance to relax on the premises.

In the interest of raising morale and sustaining employee loyalty, there are Ping-Pong tables, a poolroom, outdoor basketball court, gymnasium, bistros, soft-drink dispensaries, and facilities for film screenings, yoga practice, and Foosball. That's not counting the many getting-away-from-it-all places where, without leaving the property, employees can sit under a leafy tree or on the barbecue-equipped terrace while accompanied by a laptop.

Overall, the palette is neutral, composed of charcoal gray carpeting, white walls, silvery paneling and ductwork, plus bright accents. At workstations, tonalities of panel fabrics identify the several "neighborhoods."

As this project finished, (the job took approximately ten months, most of the time spent on upgrading power/HVAC equipment for database needs and building the mezzanines), design of 100,000 square feet (9,290 square meters) on the fourteenth floor, also assigned to The Phillips Group, began to take shape. And if that's not enough, the firm is also providing architectural services for new DoubleClick offices in Chicago, San Francisco, London, and Dublin.

Top Left: The newly-created mezzanine is basically two platforms linked by bridges and propped by columns matching those on lower floors.

Top Right: At the center of the boulevard, the park area includes seating and live Ficus trees.

Above: One of four meeting rooms.

The twelfth-floor eatery has a vaguely sigmoid shape scored with decorative wire-mesh partitions.

Blocks of enclosed offices define the boundaries of various "neighborhoods" of workstation clusters. Due to a lack of window space, ample lighting is supplemented with three new skylights.

According to the client mandate, as the **East Coast flagship for a national advertising agency** that specializes in Internet and interactive marketing packages for **Fortune 500 companies,** the office space for **Eagle River Interactive**

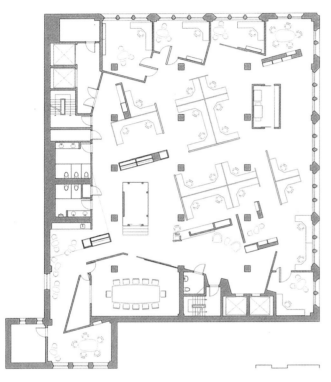

had to establish the company's presence and identity in New York. Credit for the manifestation of this project directive goes to the New York City-based firm of D'Aquino Monaco, and specifically partner-in-charge Francine Monaco and project architect Nathanial Worden. Since 1978, the firm has been responsible for corporate facilities, photo studios, art galleries, advertising agencies, and Internet design firms as well as numerous residential projects throughout New York, Connecticut, Pennsylvania, and Florida. Their directive: "It is the unique level of collaboration within the D'Aquino Monaco office, informed by the staff's various backgrounds in architecture and interiors, that have led the firm to conceive of designs integrating all scales and programs as well as interpreting any required style." The architects continue to state that "from spare Modernist office space to Neo-Victorian eclecticism, we operate without allowing anxiety about a signature look to interfere with the client's aesthetic and desired plans. Each client is addressed individually and the unique requirement of their project becomes the guiding force behind the firm's design."

The underlying organizational element of Eagle River Interactive's office layout, conceived of as a Baroque city plan, is the orthogonal grid of the structural columns. Anchored and oriented to this system are the computer and copy rooms, which, as the twin buildings of production, are conceived of as "temples within plazas," say the architects. Overlaid on the grid is a system of oblique angles upon which are oriented monolithic screening elements, light boxes, and peripheral spaces. Also oriented along this diagonal system is the "urban fabric" of the modular office furniture. The monoliths create separate zones without dividing the overall space and provide a spatial network of supports for the workstations. The monoliths also provide storage and shelving spaces, and in one case, a floor-to-ceiling whiteboard wall used by the design team to develop ideas. The four-and-a-half-foot-high (1.4-meter) light boxes of aluminum and acrylic mark the edges of a shifted grid of paths that weave between and among the columns.

6 ELEVATION - COPY ROOM

3 ELEVATION - COPY ROOM

⊗ As shown in the floor plan, the underlying organizational element of Eagle River Interactive's office layout, conceived of as a Baroque city plan, is the orthogonal grid of the structural columns.

⊘ Anchored and oriented to this
⊗ system are the computer and copy rooms, which, as the twin buildings of production, are conceived of as "temples within plazas." Elevation sketches of both are shown here.

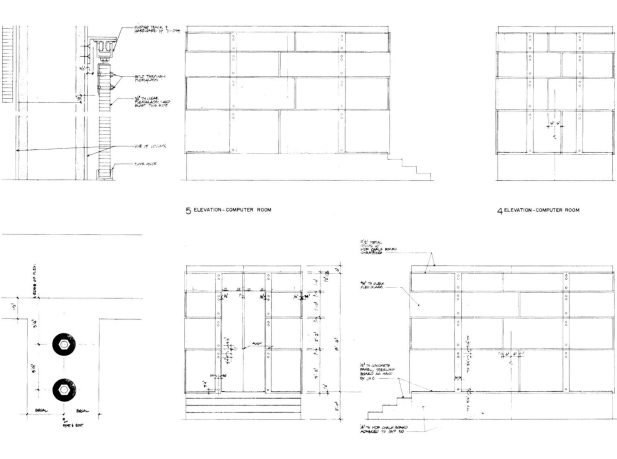

5 ELEVATION - COMPUTER ROOM   4 ELEVATION - COMPUTER ROOM

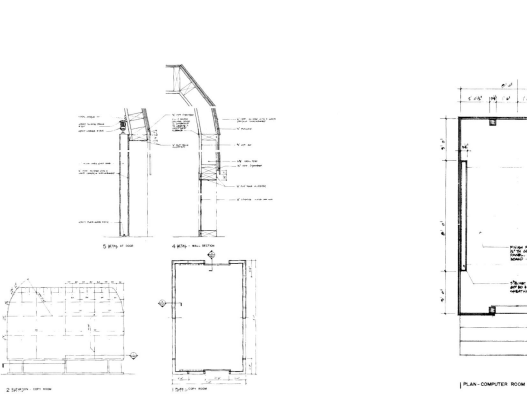

5 DETAIL AT DOOR   4 DETAIL - WALL SECTION

2 ELEVATION - COPY ROOM   1 PLAN - COPY ROOM   1 PLAN - COMPUTER ROOM

Upon entering the space, a vista opens down a diagonal boulevard focusing on the computer room, nested within an open area behind the reception desk. This plaza is bounded on one side by a 4 ft. 6 in. x 15 ft.-high (1.4 m x 4.6 m) light box, and on another side by a floor-to-ceiling monolith, which also incorporates storage. The computer room itself is a luminescent box of sandblasted acrylic that sits on a thirty-inch-high (76-centimeter) plinth clad in chalkboard. Each wall of the room is composed of a pattern of 3/4-inch-thick (1.9-centimeter) panels that float independently of one another; the one-inch (3-centimeter) gap between panels allows limited and intermittent views of the computer equipment within. Facing the computer room across the boulevard is the conference room, one wall of which slides back to give access. The opposite wall of the conference room is draped in a light bronze parachute cloth. Lit from behind, this curtain gives the illusion of an exterior window.

Another diagonal boulevard links the computer room and the copy room. The copy room reverses the material scheme of the computer room, with a luminous base and opaque walls. The upper part of the copy room is sheathed in an ascending pattern of gradually diminishing chalkboard shingles, each of which is fastened with a stainless-steel bolt.

Providing a backdrop to one side of the space are executive offices. Two of the offices have full-height facades and feature 4 ft. x 10 ft. (1.2 m x 3 m) pivoting doors. The façade of the third office is divided horizontally by a deep overhanging soffit and has a sliding wall in place of a door.

The free communication and access between all spaces in the office reflects the open, dynamic relationship between the various departments as well as the relationship between Eagle River Interactive and its clients. The image of the office is at once bold and playful, elegant and tailored.

⊘ The monoliths create separate zones without dividing the overall space, and provide a spatial network of supports for the workstations as well as storage and shelving spaces.

⊘ The computer room, a luminescent box of sandblasted acrylic, sits on a thirty-inch-high (76-centimeter) plinth. Each wall of the room is composed of a pattern of 3/4-inch-thick (1.9-centimeter) panels that float independently of one another; the one-inch (3-centimeter) gap between panels allows limited and intermittent views of the computer equipment within.

⬙ Two of the executive offices have full-height facades and feature 4 ft. x 10 ft. (1.2 m x 3 m) pivoting doors.

eEmerge was established by one of New York City's largest building owners, SL Green, to provide fractional office space **for new media and high-tech start-up companies.** The New York-based firm **NBBJ** was hired to design

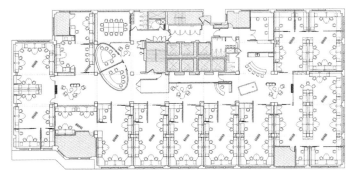

eEmerge, established by one of New York City's largest building owners, SL Green, provides fractional office space for new media and high-tech start-up companies.

a "fully wired and serviced working environment, allowing tenants to remain focused on the intense and critical aspects of their start-up business," say the design team, made up of design principal Timothy Johnson, process leader Mark Truisi, interior designer Cindy Moraza, digital designer Reggie Aviles, and designers Qui Thach and Christine Dzus. This "incubator" environment fosters a sense of creative and entrepreneurial spirit through its many shared interactive spaces such as multimedia rich meeting/break-out rooms and human interactive spaces like the coffee bar and billiards area.

Conceptually, the organization of the floor is divided into two zones: the concentrated work zone, which includes nine office suites, and the interactive zone with core support areas including meeting rooms, coffee bar, and break-out areas. Due to the building's initial use as a garment manufacturing facility, the sizable elevator core is offset from the center of the floor, thus driving the loft style layout with an open-plan exposure to all three sides. The design takes advantage of this by wrapping the core support functions around the linear core, therefore pushing the "work zone" spaces to the more valuable perimeter space. This planning move guarantees that each inhabitant has access to the perimeter and natural light.

The image of the space is formal and primary with the use of pure geometric forms and vivid color such as cadmium red and yellow. The overall organization of the floor is stabilized by a red "smart" wall, which runs continuously throughout the interactive zone and connects a multitude of functions such as break-out spaces, the elliptical Idea Room (I-Room for short), the glass-enclosed server room, reception area, and coffee bar. The use of a pure oval defining the I-Room penetrates the smart wall and is covered with dry-erase wall covering, therefore acting as a continuous writing surface, a prerequisite for any start-up company.

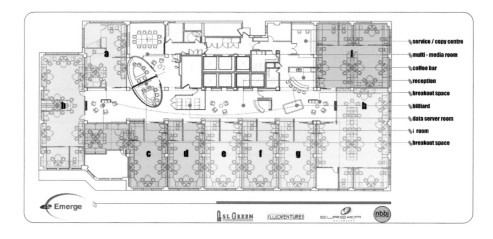

service / copy centre
multi - media room
coffee bar
reception
breakout space
billiard
data server room
i room
breakout space

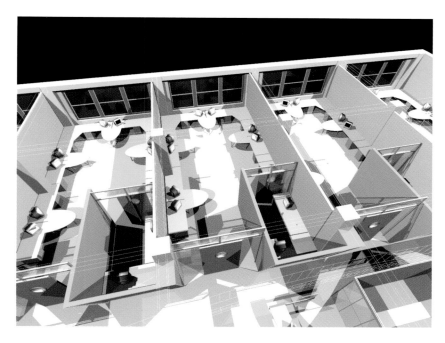

Each suite is subsequently subdivided to include both enclosed offices, typically necessary for founding partners and information-sensitive users, and open and flexible workspace to hold a higher density of digital users.

The interactive space is designed with a true sense of openness, synergy, and collaboration promoted by the mobile and informal organization of furnishings and technology. Reconfigurable break-out areas are formed around "digital" fireplaces complete with a thirty-six-inch plasma screen capable of transmitting the users' website at the snap of a cord. Full connectivity throughout the floor allows anyone to spontaneously connect to the digital world beyond.

⊘ NBBJ designed a fully wired and serviced working environment that fosters a sense of creative and entrepreneurial spirit through its many shared interactive spaces such as meeting/break-out rooms and human interactive spaces like the coffee bar and billiards area.

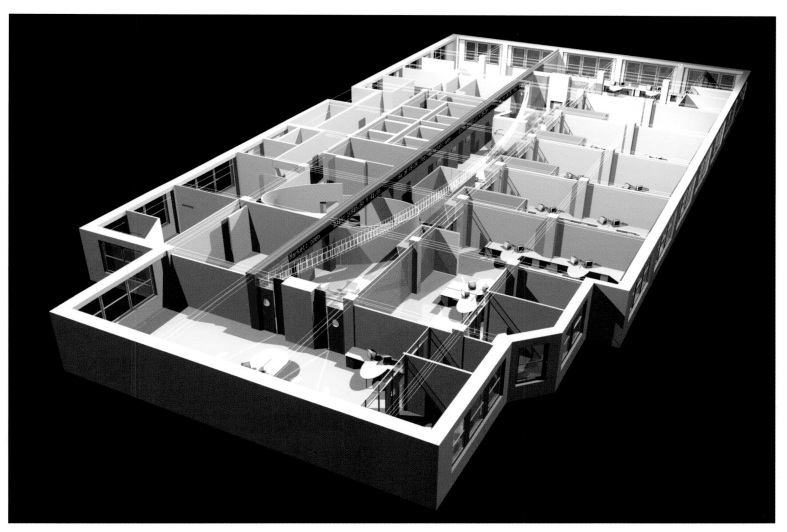

Top: The overall organization of the floor is stabilized by a red "smart" wall, which runs continuously throughout the interactive zone and connects a multitude of functions such as these break-out spaces.

Bottom Left: The floor is divided into two zones, including the concentrated work zone, which includes nine office suites, one of which is shown here.

Bottom Right: The interactive zone with core support areas includes meeting rooms, one of which is shown here, a coffee bar, and break-out areas.

⊗ Top: The reception area includes a thirty-six-inch plasma screen with the company logo.

⊗ Bottom: The interactive space includes reconfigurable break-out areas that are formed around "digital" fireplaces complete with a thirty-six-inch plasma screens.

⊗ A glass-enclosed server room provides a focal point to the reception/waiting area.

Under the **leadership** of company vice president Nicolas Ehrling and the local firms Lomar Architects and Scheiwiller Svensson Architects, **EHPT, an independent software vendor**

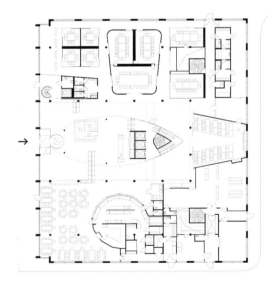

EHPT, an independent software vendor owned jointly by Ericsson and Hewlett-Packard, recently completed their Stockholm headquarters on Lindhagensgatan, which is currently being planned as a picturesque avenue with numerous new office buildings.

owned jointly by Ericsson and Hewlett-Packard, recently completed their headquarters in the northwestern area of Stockholm. Close to the city center and important traffic routes for those traveling to Arlanda and Bromma airports, the street, Lindhagensgatan, is currently being planned as a picturesque avenue with numerous new office buildings, and the entire area is poised for development over the next few years.

EHPT, established in 1993, employs more than one thousand people with offices in Europe, Asia, and the Americas. Since the company's revenue has grown by 35 percent each year and the customer's focus on the need for quick technological responses, the offices had to reflect this pacing with state-of-the-art support systems. The plan was accomplished with a simplified scheme, one that relies on architectural concepts, interior design, and facility services.

The building entrance welcomes visitors with an impressive glass variation of a magnificent classical façade. This is supported by a loggia with columns made of rust-proof steel, which clearly marks the interplay between the outside rooms and the open rooms in the atrium. The other façades are rather simple in light stucco with a base of natural stone and glass. Above the somewhat smaller penthouse floor, a boat-formed glass body rises up through the glass ceiling of the atrium. The glass façade attracts attention but also draws attention to the work going on inside the building. This openness not only gives the business an advertising function, but also lets daylight in to the large office landscape. The primary concern is openness, a unified building that is created to facilitate formal and informal meetings between employees. Around the open entrance is the restaurant, lecture halls, meeting rooms for customers, a gym, and the caretaker's office.

In contrast to the traditional office landscape, an office is created where certain functions are clearly divided so as not to disturb individuals working in their areas. In the hub of the building, with each floor raised one and a half feet (.5 m) to ensure a view, the concentration is on meeting and relaxation as well as some special work areas. This is also where the main staircase and elevators are located. Shipping, technical space, and sixty parking spots in the underground garage are in the basement.

The primary idea behind the design scheme is openness, facilitating formal and informal meetings between employees.

Apart from the polished marble floor in the atrium, the building floor is made of oiled oak. The color and material concepts—simple and light—follows the interior design theme, developed in collaboration with Sandell Sandberg. Various bridges connect work areas from one side of the building to the other. Five hundred individual workstations have been specially developed by Unifor and several particular areas have also been developed such as think rooms, communication centers, and energy rooms.

As EHPT continues to grow and develop its technological reputation, the design scheme can be replicated with modifications to ensure global coverage and local presence. It has already been implemented in nearby Gothenbrug (nine hundred workstations), Denver (seventy workstations), Grenoble (one hundred twenty workstations), and London (fifty workstations) with ongoing projects continuing to develop in Dallas, Sao Paulo, Kuala Lumpur, and New Delhi.

 Interior bridges connect work areas.

Top Right: Around the open entrance is the restaurant, an open area for employees to have informal gatherings.

⊘ Above, Right and Bottom Right
⊘ (previous page): Custom workstations from Unifor line the
perimeters of each floor.

In May 1999, Eisner Communications, a leading advertising and public relations company, moved into **the recently renovated historic Bagby Building** in Baltimore. The agency has been in Baltimore **for more than seventy years,**

⊘ Above and Top (facing page): The 50,000-square-foot (4,645-square-meter) corporate offices are located in the historic landmark Bagby Building.

and has remained at the head of its industry through close attention to its clients' branding and marketing issues. The building houses Eisner's 50,000-square-foot (4,645-square-meter) corporate headquarters, integrating its advertising, public relations, and new media groups into one space that includes offices, TV studio space, creative studios, focus group rooms, and meeting facilities.

The Bagby Furniture Company Building, constructed in 1902, was once home to one of the city's oldest furniture manufacturing companies. Located in the heart of Inner Harbor East at the foot of the Little Italy neighborhood, the building is a landmark in what has become a dynamic zone of redevelopment. Originally a four-story manufacturing facility constructed of masonry bearing walls and timber framing, the building totaled approximately 90,000 square feet (8,361 square meters) of space. An adjacent steel and corrugated sheet metal construction housed a one-story wood-drying kiln. In the 1960s, a two-story concrete masonry structure was added at the rear, bringing the total area to 100,000 square feet (9,290 square meters). The manufacturing of furniture was phased out in the 1940s, and the building became the main retail showroom space for The Bagby Furniture Company until 1990, when the business closed. Several proposals for renovating the building were developed, including housing plans, but none proceeded due to neighborhood resistance. Finally in 1996, Gensler was commissioned to renovate the building as a historically significant modern office building.

The project blends the old and the new, maintaining the building's authentic architectural character while contrasting the new uses of the building. Because Eisner Communications, the building's primary tenant, wanted to place the Bagby Building on the National Historic Register, the renovation work had to be consistent with National Park Service guidelines for the rehabilitation of historic structures. For example, existing windows were meticulously surveyed and either repaired or replaced with new units to match. The historic preservation authorities reviewed all exterior changes in detail, and the building is now part of the Register. Materials and spaces are highly responsive to the three different types of buildings—the warehouse, the kiln building, and the concrete masonry building.

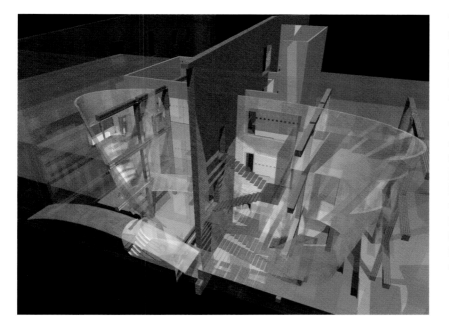

The character of the existing structure was expressed by designing the interior spaces to expose the floor framing and brick walls. An adjoining loading area became a courtyard and second entrance for the building. Between the two-story masonry portion and the main Bagby building, an additional floor and light filled atrium formed an effective transition space.

The Bagby Building presented Gensler with many additional design opportunities. Gensler designed the interiors for the two primary tenants of the building, Eisner Communications and Caliber Learning Network, and developed historically accurate typefaces for the building's exterior painted banner signage. To create an identifiable entry, designers incorporated a canopy on the Exeter Street façade and a monumental stair in Eisner's main lobby. The kiln building was preserved and completely renovated to become office space and potential retail space. New cores, two elevators, and new mechanical, electrical, and life safety systems completed the renovations.

Eisner Communications' headquarters includes offices, TV studio space, creative studios, focus group rooms, and formal and informal meeting facilities.

For Eisner Communications' interior, evolving team structure required better, more creative work patterns to foster collaboration. Further, Eisner sought to develop a "brand factory" where account teams would be fully immersed in their clients' brand and marketing worlds as well as their own day-to-day operations. These congruous goals heavily influenced the spatial organization of the workplace. Gensler designed four major hubs for the brand factories. Each centered offices and open-work areas surround a large scaffold structure that acts as a flexible billboard, brainstorm center, and expression of the team's mission. Multiple scales of work environments were created for flexibility and adaptability. Textured materials such as translucent fiberglass walls, medium density fiberboard, and rubber flooring, together with industrial lighting, kept costs low while adding a unique feel to the spaces.

Designers maximized daylight penetration deep into the space. High floor-to-floor heights permitted partitions to float clear of structure, so light reaches even the innermost areas. New atria were cut out of the existing space, and all windows were either refurbished or replaced. Areas of the floor are made of glass block to create glowing destination points at the end of various hallways. Designers created a new mezzanine space on the fifth floor, providing a view of Baltimore's Inner Harbor neighborhoods.

Part of Eisner Communications' intent of moving into this historic building was to retain its authentic, high-touch feeling, a contrast with the high-tech work that the agency is producing. Gensler worked closely within this ideal to express the company's philosophy of blending the old and the new, enforcing Eisner Communications' position as an established yet innovative agency through the design.

To create an identifiable entry, Gensler designers incorporated a canopy on the Exeter Street façade and a monumental stair in Eisner Communications' main lobby.

Gensler sketch of offices with open work areas surrounded by a scaffold structure that can be used as a brainstorm area.

For years, **Euro RSG Tatham,** one of the largest advertising agencies around, **had a prestigious address** on the corner **of North Michigan Avenue and Oak Street.**

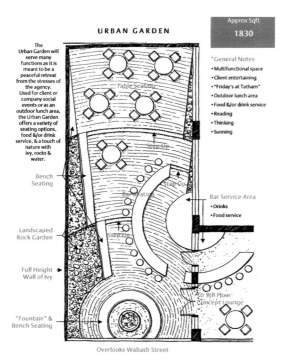

URBAN GARDEN

Approx Sqft
1830

The Urban Garden will serve many functions as it is meant to be a peaceful retreat from the stresses of the agency. Used for client or company social events or as an outdoor lunch area, the Urban Garden offers a variety of seating options, food &/or drink service, & a touch of nature with ivy, rocks & water.

Bench Seating

Landscaped Rock Garden

Full Height Wall of Ivy

"Fountain" & Bench Seating

Table Seating

Step Up

Bar Seating

Step Up

Step Up

To 9th Floor Concept Lounge

*General Notes
• Multifunctional space
• Client entertaining
• "Friday's at Tatham"
• Outdoor lunch area
• Food &/or drink service
• Reading
• Thinking
• Sunning

Bar Service Area
• Drinks
• Food service

Overlooks Wabash Street

⊘ Space created an urban garden for the Euro RSG Tatham offices, a peaceful retreat from agency stress.

The offices were clad in mahogany and granite—rich, luscious, and stuffy. For their new offices, the company decided to celebrate their creativity and selected two floors and a roof deck/urban garden in an unconventional five-floor high rise off Michigan Avenue. The company conducted a standard interviewing process for design firms all around the country but with one twist. At the eleventh hour, SPACE, the Chicago-based design firm, was asked to create a rendering of what a new reception area would look like. For a firm that prides itself on a dynamic programming effort, the design team at SPACE felt uncomfortable developing any ideas without client input. Instead, says Dana Hegedorn, the project's design director, the team created a deck of cards with a Rorschach ink blot test on the cover with the question "Reception, what does it mean to you?" "Each card had a reception concept," says Hegedorn, "from image to style to color to functionality. The last card emphasized that the firm will provide you with a reception area, but cannot tell you what it looks like until we work together." That idea won SPACE the job.

The design process began with SPACE conducting focus groups organized by department. All members of Euro RSG Tatham were encouraged to participate. These sessions gave individuals and departments an opportunity to express their requirements and wishes pertaining to the new workplace philosophy, organization, workspace standards, and support areas. Resulting data informed SPACE of functional requirements and also aesthetic direction.

Two major concepts affecting the workplace emerged from the focus groups. The first issue confronted whether organizing the staff by department (i.e., business development, creative, research, production, etc.) or by team produced the highest degree of productivity. Almost unanimously, it was felt that organization by department offered the most benefits. Information exchange, sharing of resources, personnel back up, and a sense of camaraderie are some of these benefits.

The second issue dealt with the gains of an open-office versus a private-office culture. Those currently in a private office feared that moving to an open workspace would sacrifice privacy and the ability to focus thus decreasing performance. Specifically targeting confidentiality and personal privacy as casualties of an open-office environment, it was felt that any gains of interaction an open office offered could be achieved by bringing meetings out of private offices and into common areas. Interestingly, those who currently reside in open workspaces did not request offices. They focused on improving the function of open workspaces. More layout space, improved ergonomic conditions, and more privacy were some other requests.

THIRD & FOURTH FLOOR

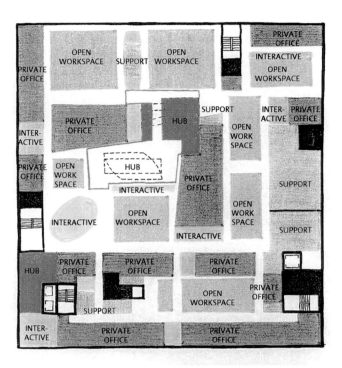

OHIO STREET

GRAND AVENUE

WABASH AVENUE

ADJACENCIES

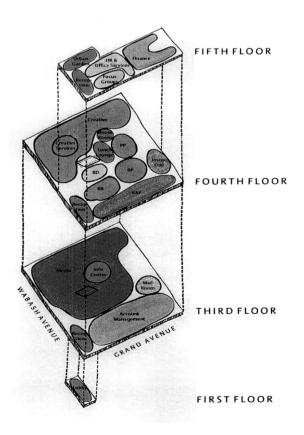

FIFTH FLOOR

FOURTH FLOOR

THIRD FLOOR

FIRST FLOOR

These issues were brought to the attention of the core group early in the programming process. The core team strategized to create as many offices as the plan would allow without sacrificing aesthetic or flow. It was also decided to organize the staff by department recognizing the economics of shared resources.

With eighteen-foot-high (5.5-meter) ceilings, few windows in new buildings, and a giant floor plate—two floors that add up to 40,000 square feet (3,716 square meters)—SPACE was able to create a dramatic theatrical feeling with light and a scheme based on channel surfing. Creating a variety of venues for people to work in and experience as visitors walk through the office, the design team developed a series of sporadic images throughout the space. "Everywhere you look," says Hegedorn, "there is something new, a colored wall, open space, small meeting rooms." Everything—from the lunchroom, open meeting spaces, information areas, conference room with lounge seating, and steps up to roof deck—radiates from a central area that is designated as a red cone.

The new private offices were reduced in size so meetings could occur in more common areas; meeting room sizes were enlarged. "People are out and about," says Hegedorn. "You can see activity everywhere." Integrating technology into the new space became a priority and the presentation room has televisions of various sizes to show off various campaigns and ad ideas. The room's configuration can be changed based on a mood or client need. SPACE hired an exhibit designer to install a pipe system that can attach cart rails, stereo, speakers, televisions, etc. The exposed equipment is flexible not formal.

The design team at SPACE collaborated with their client to create a new type of workspace that succeeds in connecting with company-wide goals and needs. Throughout the process, employees were encouraged to exchange ideas and input, resulting in an environment that works for everyone.

The third and fourth floors of Euro RSG Tatham's new office include private and open work-spaces as well as interactive areas for meetings both formal and informal.

After winning the project by not pre-designing the reception area, SPACE worked with the client to create an entry that works with the company ideals.

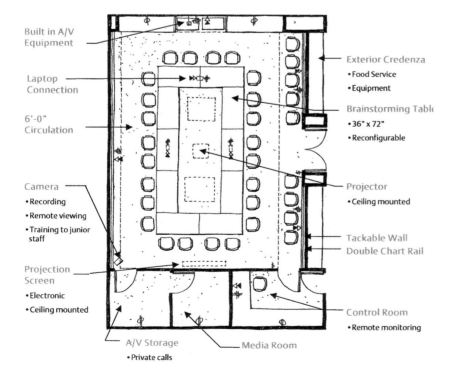

Built in A/V
Equipment

Laptop
Connection

6'-0"
Circulation

Camera
• Recording
• Remote viewing
• Training to junior
  staff

Projection
Screen
• Electronic
• Ceiling mounted

A/V Storage

Media Room
• Private calls

Exterior Credenza
• Food Service
• Equipment

Brainstorming Table
• 36" x 72"
• Reconfigurable

Projector
• Ceiling mounted

Tackable Wall
Double Chart Rail

Control Room
• Remote monitoring

Private offices, glass enclosed to encourage communication, were reduced in size so meetings could occur in more common areas.

Left and Bottom (previous page): In the presentation room, an exhibit designer installed a pipe system that can attach cart rails, stereo, speakers, televisions, etc.

As the old adage goes, "Image is everything"

and today, it is even more apropos in the fast-paced digital era. So when an Atlanta-based software company wanted a **dramatic presentation room** within its corporate headquarters,

A theatrical-looking wood portal frames the transition from the entry vestibule to the display gallery, where neon and color-filtered light illuminates a sheer silver Knoll Textiles drapery, which provides a backdrop for video/data monitors and display pedestals.

their design scheme required a combination of high-tech and high-style, and TVS Interiors delivered. The Atlanta-based firm, a corporate affiliate of Thompson, Ventulett, Stainback & Associates, Inc., built the company's headquarters and knew well that the design team, which included Lucy Aiken-Johnson, senior associate/project manager Nancy Cartledge, as well as principal Steven Clem, and project designer Gina Zastrow, could create an unusual and evocative facility. TVS Interiors' portfolio includes corporate projects, convention centers, retail facilities, store planning, and hospitality; all of this experience aided in developing the final design scheme for the executive presentation theater, one that is distinctive, futuristic, and sleek. The theater, a showplace where vision and strategy for the company is presented to potential customers, includes a variety of display areas for nearly sixty software solutions, as well as state-of-the-art audio/visual equipment and a Data Center. TVS Interiors sought to develop an experience, synchronized by audio, video, and lighting, which would emotionally and physically navigate the customer through a story of the industry's past, present, and future.

Typically, visitors are ushered through the theater by a pair of presenters, whose tours are finely choreographed to include an elaborate sequence of lighting scenes and audio/visual effects that are designed to create a "Wow" response. In partnership with TVS Interiors, lighting designers from Ramon Luminance Design

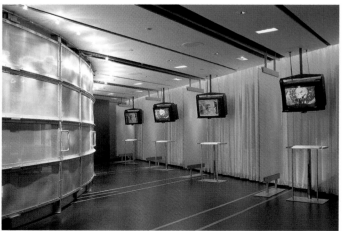

In the display gallery, the sheer silver drapery shimmers in the glow of the video monitors and presents a dramatic appearance. Stainless-steel wire cloth panels house cable lighting.

created the theatrical presentation along with audio/visual and acoustical engineers from Lee Sound Design and installers Technical Industries, Inc.

Upon entering the 3,250-square-foot space (292.5-square-meters), visitors gather in the entry vestibule, which displays print ads and product brochures. A dramatic wood portal frames the transition to the display gallery. Here, the backdrop for display pedestals and video/data monitors is sheer silver Knoll Textiles drapery illuminated by neon and color-filtered lighting. The theatrical setting instantly lets visitors know what is in store. Stainless-steel wire cloth panels, which serve as the theater walls, act as a scrim for cable lighting from Translite Systems. All custom metal fixtures are provided by locals Fabmaster, Inc., and custom millwork from Mortenson Woodwork, Inc.

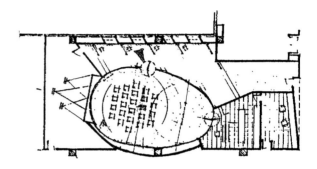

The pivoting door provides access to the theater from the display gallery. The stainless-steel cloth panels appear transparent or opaque depending upon the illumination, to reveal or conceal the theater space.

A large pivoting door provides dramatic entry into the high-tech and comfortable theater space that is enclosed within the stainless-steel cloth panels. Inside the theater, leather upholstered chairs and incandescent lighting contrast greatly with the cool exterior, giving the theater a warm atmosphere.

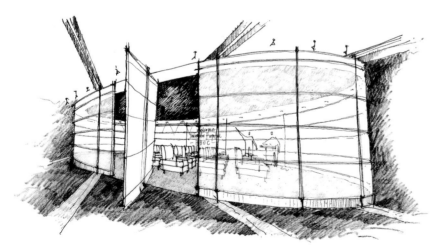

As the story progresses, the neon color changes to red and the stainless-steel screen enclosure is illuminated to reveal the interior of a 25-seat theater space. A large, pivoting door allows visitors access to comfortable and plush lounge seating from Metro. Leather upholstery, wood finishes, and incandescent lighting contrast with the coolness of the gallery finishes; elliptical curves throughout the design scheme welcome and embrace visitors. Once customers are seated, motorized screen panels reveal a multimedia presentation. Custom-built lecterns and a large-format 10-foot-by-16-foot (3-meter-by-4.9-meter) rear screen projection system create virtual settings for the presenters to demonstrate their products in various applications and a surround-sound audio system rounds out the scene. Presenters also use a combination of prompting screens, touch panels, remote controls, and an Intelligent or Smart Board all within reach of the lecterns to further enhance the presentations.

From the back area of the theater, the Data Center orchestrates portions of the presentation. The story concludes when the theater lights dim within the main theater and the Oz Data Center, as it is affectionately known, demonstrates the efficiencies of specific product applications.

As a marketing and selling tool, TVS Interiors' executive presentation theater has won rave reviews from company employees; presenters are able to convey a progressive, up-to-date (and beyond) image to prospective clients and visitors. Within the corporate headquarters, the client can show off their vision and strategy in a dramatic fashion. And, as the competition heats up in the software industry, the client can rest assured that they are one step ahead of their rivals.

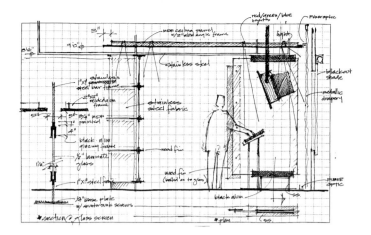

◈ The original sketches for the display gallery includes technical information about certain materials and products that are used to exhibit industry information.

◇ The overall floor plan of the executive theater space offers a complete view of the 3,250-square-foot (292.5-square-meters) facility, showing the plan of the display gallery outside the theater, as well as other office space.

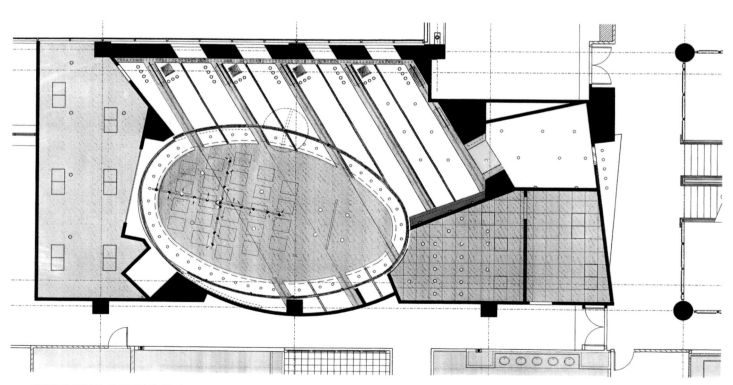

REFLECTED CEILING PLAN

The actual theater space is appointed with warm leather upholstery and wood finishes as well as a 10-foot-by-16-foot (3-meter-by-4.9-meter) rear projection screen for presentations.

The information technology firm **Fluidminds** wanted to create an **appealing work environment** and decided on a 500-square-meter (5,382-square-foot) loft **in Stockholm**

near Kungsholstorg Square for the facility. The company, a management consultancy group with an ambition to be different from the competition, is driven by a passion to realize changes others talk about and make clients achieve goals they dream about. Founded in September 1998, Fluidminds has since taken a leading position as the spokesmen for the New Economy, and its client list includes both large and small companies. When Fluidminds decided to move into new premises in central Stockholm, they also wanted to entice other small firms to join them. The interior design was crucial for demonstrating what the members of the network shared in common.

In the competition it ran for "the best meeting place for 50 people," appropriately called The Stable, Ursing Architects' Bureau won. "Ursing's solution takes advantage of the three-dimensional space of the premises," says Michael Daun, CEO of Fluidminds, "giving it the sense of openness we were looking for." The Stockholm-based architecture/design firm created a new concept—highly flexible space meant to promote tailored customer communication. Ursing combines the virtues of an open-space design—fluidity, economy in the use of floor space, and mobile work areas—with the cozy atmosphere of smaller balconies to form a coherent whole.

The design team at Ursing Architects Bureau, led by principal Jacob Ursing, asked themselves "How do you design offices for a company that talks about a future where we wear computer chips in our shoes and that occasionally uses open-floor spaces in its working areas for maneuvering remote-controlled cars?" The client also mandated a functional open space that would enable people to meet more often and do more things together in uncramped quarters. At the same time, the client wanted to keep the sound volume low and conversation confidential.

Functionality had top priority, but the company also described in detail what type of moods were compatible with the "stable dwellers" style of working and communicating with their customers. "I wanted to create a unified space combining maximal openness with strong and specific moods for the smaller work modules," says Ursing. "What we have arrived at today is an optimally functioning office premise combining traditional concepts of flexibility with atmospheric work corners, a space that interacts efficiently with its environment."

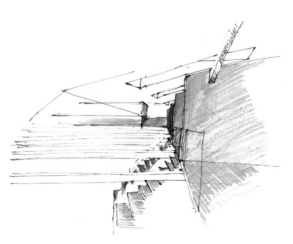

Ursing's design for Fluidminds provides creative space for 50 employees.

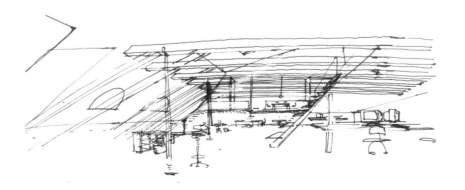

Ursing wanted to capture the combination of playfulness and professionalism that attracts customers to the network. Their new workspaces maximize the meeting and cooperation among the different companies while simultaneously profiling them in common to the world outside. As company president Michael Daun explains: "Playfulness, creativity, and idiosyncrasy are all elements in our business strategy. And in our world, that represents no contradiction to professionalism. This office space should be the materialization of our manifesto."

Lighting was an important consideration—the premises had few windows, except for some dormers. To bring daylight into the conference rooms, the design of the lanterns was changed and enlarged. Illumination has been thoroughly considered, both functionally and in terms of stage setting. At the same time, Ursing decided to make the lighting as intensive as that in a commercial store in order to create the feeling of energy.

Architectural solutions were based on Fluidminds' ideas about how they wanted to work; how they wanted to sit in order to avoid establishing hierarchical territories; and how the spatial layout should encourage movement and communication among the companies. Fluidminds has acquired an open work zone combined with several quiet, isolated rooms and Ursing designed small worktables in organic shapes with feathered edges, like leaves floating in the room. To make further use of the available area and to create more space, the team located the separate conference rooms on the mezzanine floor.

A series of staircases lead up to the mezzanine level, where separate conference rooms are located.

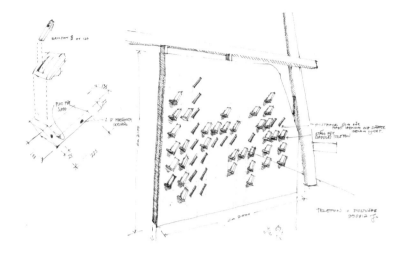

"The flexible office," where the employees move among fixed workstations, became the modern approach to office design in Sweden during the 90s, but Ursing felt that in reality these design schemes are often boring and anonymous variations on the office landscapes of the 70s. What distinguished Fluidminds' layout is an even greater degree of flexibility aided by portable tools combined with a vision of its premises as a landscape of different regions and practicable workspaces. People are able to get together in the vestibule or the cafeteria just as easily as at one of the worktables. The space has a totally wireless network, and the computers have LAN PC cards facilitating Intranet communications. Ursing also achieved this multiplicity of work possibilities by creating spaces with different characters and opportunities rather than individual workstations. One example of this is selection of the primary colors, furnishings, and electrical appliances in six different conference rooms to reinforce the character of each room. The magenta color and the round shapes of the furnishings were selected to achieve an unalloyed space in which to think clearly. In the light orange room, there is a gray, austere table because this is a serious room for cool, rational decisions. One of the more informal meeting places is a green sofa fixed to the wall in the lounge on the mezzanine floor. Around the low coffee table there are stuffed footstools in bright colors. This place was created with the importance of informal space for business relations and conversations in mind.

"We work in close proximity to one another; we're always on the run; and we move from place to place to get new ideas and avoid getting stuck in a pattern," says Daun. "There is a built-in dynamic in these premises—you're never more than two steps from a conversation. If you like that kind of interaction, then these premises are ideal."

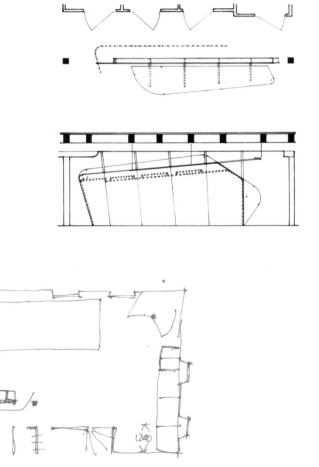

⊗ This informal greeting space is
intended for social and business
interaction.

⊗ Ursing Architect's original sketches and elevation plans.

Although the story is an old, familiar one by now, it begs to be repeated in the case of **Funny Garbage.** Founded on a very tight shoestring budget in 1995,

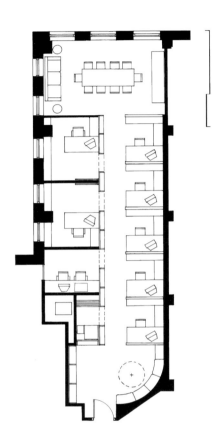

the company has grown into one of New York's hottest media design companies and web development businesses with a client list that includes Cartoon Network, Nike, and David Byrne. For the company's first office in New York City, partner Peter Girardi asked Specht Harpman to create a space with limited resources but unlimited creativity. At one point, Girardi even gave a vague description of the space he wanted to see: "make it look crappy." Oddly familiar with this kind of request, the experts Scott Specht and Louise Harpman merged affordability and innovation and constructed the 1,200-square-foot (111-square-meter) office in no time.

First, like many firms today working on a tight deadline, Specht Harpman rethought the traditional relationship between designer, client, and contractor. Rather than pricing out the entire project, the firm priced individual tasks so Funny Garbage could decide whether to do things on a case-by-case basis. Supplies were collected from local sources and transported by truck. And, in a state of design congeniality, both designers as well as company staff and friends donated part-time labor. When something could not be bought, the designers made or found it. Staples provided the file cabinets. Wood and metal chairs, found abandoned by a midtown Manhattan sweatshop, were pulled from a dumpster to provide conference room seating.

◉ A full illustration for the 1,200-square-foot (111-square-meter) office space.

◉ A three-dimensional representation of the Funny Garbage offices.

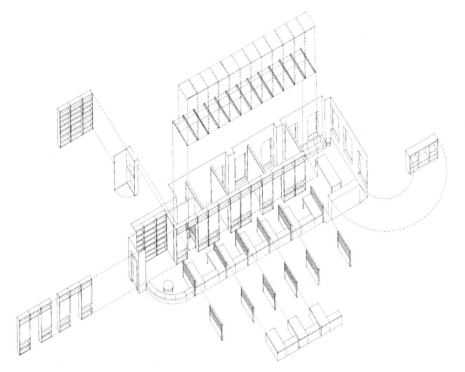

With the able-bodied help of design assistant Amy Lopez-Cepero, the architects developed a scheme that lines the central passageway with semiprivate workspaces on either side. This proved efficient and created a more open space because the flanking layers of transparent screen partly enclosed the spaces. To encourage employee interaction, the offices have porous walls and no doors. Originally, the company partners at Funny Garbage wanted private offices at the rear of the space. However, the designers quickly persuaded them to place a conference/meeting room there because of the great light and fantastic views. Now, the entire office can share in the good design fortune.

Keeping in mind the "crappy" scheme, Specht and Harpman chose a palette of industrial materials with an emphasis on non-color. Using the materials in a most clever way, a recycled steel angled shelving unit, a prominent design element, creates a long screen wall, distinguishing space and creating storage and display areas. Attached to the shelving are sheets of Masonite and panels of perforated steel left unfinished so that they will rust over time. Above the main passageway, the perforated metal forms a cantilevered canopy that gives spatial definition and hides the messy plaster ceiling. All the while, allowing daylight to pour in from the skylight above.

In keeping within budget, the meeting area uses inexpensive, off-the-shelf and found objects.

For fun, kitsch tchotchkes are displayed around and throughout the office.

Workstations are made of solid core doors atop file cabinets, pinup surfaces, and individually controlled light boxes.

Each workstation includes solid core doors on the file cabinets, pin-up surfaces made of Homasote, and vertical light box dividing panels that can be individually controlled. All of these elements sit on a base of Durock tile backer board, a material that is usually concealed in spaces. Here, it offers a filigree of fiberglass mesh that incorporates a date of production stamp, a decorative graphic surface. All employees sit on Jacobsen chairs from ICF and the artwork came through Jean-Christophe Castelli.

The lighting scheme also mixes the off-the-shelf look with custom work. In addition to using $15 Stonco floodlights, Specht Harpman created a special light fixture for the entry and waiting areas. The two cut pie-shaped wedges of Corulite (the same material used for postal bins) and bolted them together.

With unique design gestures and new ideals, Specht Harpman has changed the way materials are used in offices and how products are created for one-of-a-kind spaces. They have proved that custom does not always mean costly. Like all good stories, this one ends on a high note. As the company continues to grow and expand, Funny Garbage has taken on two more spaces in the same building. It seems Specht Harpman is on board...again.

Specht and Harpman used a recycled steel angle shelving unit to create a long screen wall, distinguishing space and creating storage and display areas.

Top and Middle: Japanese toys from the 1960s and 1970s provide humorous diversion for employees, clients, and visitors.

Bottom: Masonite panels were attached to lower shelves as backing for books and supplies. Perforated metal panels were attached to provide a greater sense of depth, privacy, and texture.

A curved sofa sets up the waiting area; beyond, individual workstations made of Durock tie backer board and Homasote. Light boxes are made out of translucent fiberglass. Above, Specht Harpman's custom light fixture.

A perforated metal canopy hangs over the central passage, hiding the plaster ceiling. Recycled steel shelving provides a semitransparent separation between work and circulation spaces.

Recently, **ORMS,** the London-based design firm, completed a 33,000-square-foot (2,787-square-meter) fit-out for **Hill & Knowlton (UK) Limited,** the rapidly expanding international public relations company which is part of the WPP Group,

integrating the business into the building

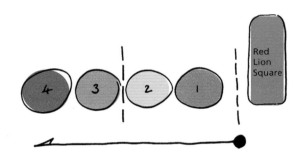

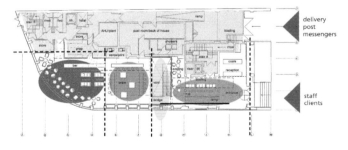

1. entrance and reception
2. impact - the catalyst
3. brain
4. café

linkages are crucial

thresholds are significant

at Red Lion Square in London. Hill & Knowlton was keen to give clients and staff an impression of how the whole company operates from the moment they walked into reception. This was achieved by opening up the ground and first floors, enabling a complete cross section of the business—the client conference rooms, the communal "Brain" and cafe areas, and a typical working floor—to be seen from one spot. A glass tread feature staircase, designed with Michael Hadi & Associates, leads down to the conference rooms.

ORMS helped Hill & Knowlton decide on the suitability of the building in London's W1 area. The low ceiling heights—6 feet 8 inches (1.8 meter 20 centimeter)—turned away all potential occupiers, but ORMS came up with an innovative solution that maximized the heights available by taking the ceiling back to shell. The existing cooling system was reused, which saved funds and kept the project within the tight budget of £2.2m. ORMS started the project with an absolutely fixed budget and program. The key question for the client was "Could we make it work?"

Hill & Knowlton wanted to create more space for communal use, which ORMS achieved by actually reducing the space per person without making them feel cramped. The result—happier staff and a much-improved working environment—is that staff turnover has reduced significantly since September 2000.

Recently, ORMS, the London-based design firm, completed a 33,000-square-foot (2,787-square-meter) fit-out for Hill & Knowlton.

Top and Bottom: With the help of the London-based firm ORMS, Hill & Knowlton were keen to give visitors an impression of how the whole company operates from the moment they walked into reception.

reception

- 'smell the energy'

- a display

- global information

- floating objects

......minimal effort/**maximum impact**

Hill + Knowlton

ORMS Architecture Design

ORMS opened up the ground and first floors enabling a complete cross section of the business—the client conference rooms, the communal "Brain" and cafe areas, and a typical working floor—to be seen from one spot.

basement conference room

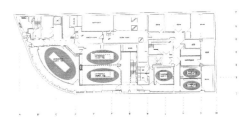

- 3 no. 16 people conference rooms
- 3 no. 6/8 people meeting rooms
- air-conditioned
- audio visual facilities
- food service

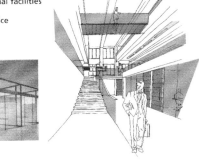

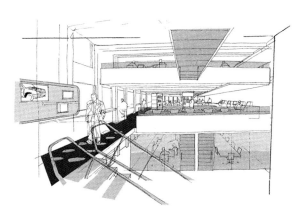

A glass tread feature staircase, designed with Michael Hadi & Associates, leads down to the conference rooms.

Hill + Knowlton

ORMS Architecture Design

The design of **Hurd Studios,** a computer animation and multimedia medical imaging company in New York's Soho district, required a **graphics animation workroom, two private offices, four semiprivate offices, a conference area,**

⊗ The graphics workroom accommodates employees who design computer animation and multimedia medical imaging.

a pantry, and a reception area. Who better than to deliver the goods but Specht Harpman, the New York-based firm thoroughly ensconced in the digital design world.

Hurd's stronghold is in rendering and animating intricately detailed bodies and body parts for pharmaceutical companies like Merck, Pfizer, Bristol-Meyers Squibb; health care organizations like the American Heart Association and the National Institute of Health; Websites like iVillage; and many other medical professionals. The stop-frame animation software employed by Hurd was a direct design influence on the scheme of the new 1,800-square-foot (167-square-meter) offices. (It is also interesting to note that a 1,000-square-foot (93-square-meter) addition is currently underway.) According to architects Scott Specht and Louise Harpman, "Hurd Studios composes its diagnostic sequences in single, meticulously rendered frames, which become fused when multiple images are animated. The dominance of the individual frame, which recedes as it becomes part of a seamless animation, inspired us to create another kind of frame system for the construction of the studio."

The interior plan is an inverted L. A square workroom connects to a long narrow corridor that includes the reception zone, storage walls, pantry, and conference area. A framing system, used throughout the space, integrates everything—from desks, walls, and doors to storage, lighting, and ductwork—and is made of translucent Primex plastic panels, cherry plywood panels, welding tab, and one-inch steel tube stock. For example, one wall lining the full length of Hurd Studios' offices is multifunctional, housing file cabinets, tack surfaces, shelving, coat closet, pantry, water cooler, ductwork with Seiho jet diffusers, and a rolling ladder by Cotterman. The framing system also encompasses a freestanding steel tube "cage" (as the designers lovingly refer to it) that contains four semiprivate offices with sliding doors. This forms a threshold into the workroom from the main corridor. In the workroom, steel tubing transforms into shelving. Along the corridor, the framing becomes an armature for seating, storage, pantry, and exposed ductwork (9944-6).

Two offices that look onto the workroom have storage carved into nearly every corner of space.

The "cage" contains four semiprivate offices that create a buffer zone between the workroom and more public spaces. Sliding doors are incorporated in the framing system.

Determined to find the best fabricators to create the apparently complicated framing system and welders to create the support system, Specht and Harpman did not have to venture far to find what they were looking for. In a most fortuitous manner, during the design process the architects moved their offices to a new location in the city's garment district and soon after discovered a local welding shop that employed highly-skilled fabricators. Like magic, the design team had found their welders.

The beauty of Specht Harpman's interior design scheme for Hurd Studios is the seemingly simple four-part construction. However, extensive steel tubing had to be drawn frame by frame by the design team and modeled to scale so that the newly-found metalworkers, who had never worked with architectural drawings, could produce the steel skeleton. And, to make matters a bit trickier, the tubing was welded off-site and assembled on-site. But the end results are an engineering feat. According to Specht Harpman, the longest stretch of framing, running thirty-eight feet (11.6 meters) along the full length of the space, was just one-quarter of an inch off the mark when installed. Specht Harpman specified a variety of different materials and products to round out the Hurd Studios' interior. From Herman Miller chairs and Allsteel file cabinets to Forbo tack surfaces, the offices project a professional appearance with expert millwork/panel scribe by Tony Sandkamp and the steel matrix by Armando Saca. For special design touches Specht Harpman custom designed a lighting fixture for the conference room and reception area and a table for the conference area. Never ones to rest on their laurels, Specht Harpman developed an interior scheme that speaks to both the client's professionalism and high-tech identity, combining an understanding of skilled design and unique details.

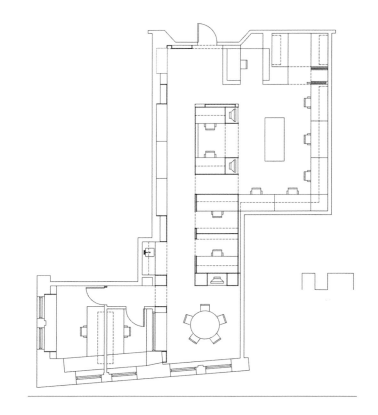

Specht Harpman created a model for the Hurd Studios project.

The "cage" contains four semiprivate offices that create a buffer zone between the workroom and more public spaces. Sliding doors are incorporated in the framing system.

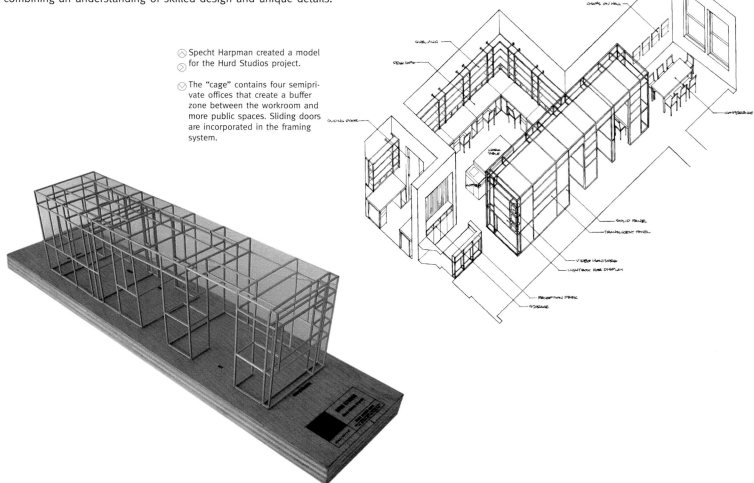

The conference room, resembling a captain's quarters or private train car, intersects with a private office and small pantry.

The desk in the reception area has a flat plate steel surface and the sconce is custom designed by Specht Harpman. Here, seating is integrated into the framing system.

Like many **new media companies, Internet**Connect, a broadband networking solutions provider for businesses in the **United States and abroad,** has had a successful run of it.

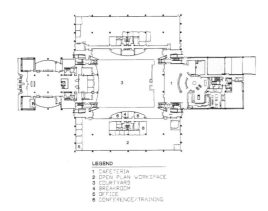

LEGEND
1 CAFETERIA
2 OPEN PLAN WORKSPACE
3 COURTYARD
4 BREAKROOM
5 OFFICE
6 CONFERENCE/TRAINING

InternetConnect's floor plan illustrates the company's 180,000-square-foot (16,722-square-meter) facility.

So much so that their growth has been measured at 1,000 percent during the past year. Due to this incredible achievement, an obvious problem occurred. The company's staff expanded and their space needs grew. To support this situation, the company signed a lease for a new 180,000-square-foot (16,722-square-meter) headquarters.

Thriving e-business is characterized by growth and making the most of every opportunity, but also of uncertainty. The process of creating workplaces for e-business must in turn be characterized by solutions that make it simpler to proceed quickly, offer agility to change quickly and often, and make it possible to seize every opportunity. The new InternetConnect headquarters is a combination of many such solutions.

Interior Space International (ISI) joined InternetConnect's project team on April 1, 2000, and structured a planning and design strategy that enabled the organization to be fully operational with new furnishings in the new facility on June 12, 2000. That's about two months—something virtually unheard of in the design world.

Staubach provided site selection and leasing consulting to Internet-Connect, assisting in achieving an "asap" relocation by identifying the one geographically acceptable facility, which already had an adequate infrastructure for lighting and building systems in place as well as a raised floor system for power/voice/data cabling. Wylie & Associates represented InternetConnect in all aspects of project management, highlighted by implementation and coordination of vast and complex cabling requirements over a period of several weeks.

New systems furniture was needed quickly, but client groups were not certain about which workstation sizes would work best. ISI and Wylie & Associates streamlined the process: a one-size-fits-all generic prototype sketch was distributed only to those manufacturers whose products could, in future, move "off module" and thus permit later low-cost change to a variety of workstation sizes. Each

Below: ISI had to install new systems furniture quickly. Working with Wylie & Associates, they found a manufacturer whose workstations could move "off module" in the future and permit later low-cost changes to size.

manufacturer responded with their rendition that best met budget considerations and the requirement to deliver and install a total of six hundred stations in six weeks. Mockups were hurriedly staged with parts on hand in local showrooms, and within two weeks design selection was complete, a purchase order signed, and fabrication and shipping underway.

Preexisting private offices were too few and large, and constructed of moveable wall components. The lead times required to order more moveable wall components exceeded the move-in date, so the design team carefully puzzled out how to relocate the fewest wall units resulting in the creation of the most additional offices. These reconfigurations also increase the penetration of sunlight into the building and create a more inviting pedestrian flow pattern throughout the complex.

The existing building was characterized by box-like space and subtle finishes from past decades. InternetConnect required instead an environment to reflect the movement and energy of a young business organization. With little time and a desire for high-impact design, the decision was made to do a great deal of painting very quickly. A dynamic palette of colors, finishes, and forms had been carried throughout the building via painted murals, columns, and systems furniture. With some wings dominated by purple and others by bright melon, painted landmark elements orient occupants and visitors as they travel around the site. One such landmark is the "C" wing's internal stair. The stair becomes a focal point for navigating through the wing. Particularly pleasurable is the experience of movement up and down the stairs, heightened by the movement of color across the walls of the surrounding space.

⬙ A total of six hundred custom workstations were delivered to InternetConnect and installed in six weeks.

◁ Forms and shapes throughout the public spaces aid in the flow and circulation.

▽ To reflect the movement and energy of a young business organization, the designers used a dynamic palette of colors and finishes throughout the building.

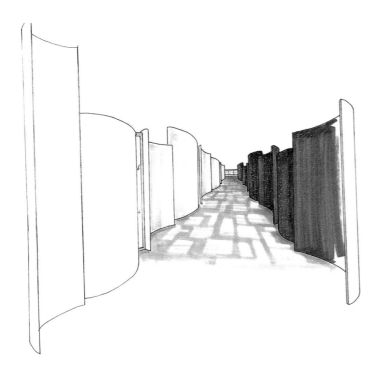

A temporary reception area was needed for the first few months of occupancy. The objective was to establish some separation between employees and the distractions of waiting visitors while enabling the visitors to be aware of the high-energy activity going on within the office space. The solution was to enclose the reception area with a sinuously draped metal mesh curtain, which glitters and both displays and obscures the bright colors and activity beyond.

Finally, a cafeteria is located in the middle of the complex, opening directly onto beautiful Japanese gardens and waterfalls. Its location is ideal as a venue for celebrating InternetConnect community spirit, providing a decompression outlet for staff, indulging in the playful aspects of the corporate culture, and experiencing the blending of indoor and outdoor space. A riot of playful colors and finishes on every surface in the cafeteria enlivened a formerly dark and dated space. A favorite spot on the campus, it has quickly become so popular that a company-wide contest is currently underway to christen it with an appropriately special name.

ISI's plan—create a dynamic palette of colors and finishes that reflects the energy and innovation of this young organization, while one-size workstations and a raised floor throughout provide ultimate flexibility for constant change at minimal cost—works well for this burgeoning company. The design scheme efficiently speaks to today's e-business needs.

The internal staircase, a focal point for navigating through the space, includes the movement of color across the walls of the surrounding space.

A bold purple was used in the reception and waiting areas to welcome visitors to a high-energy business environment.

Top: A temporary reception area is enclosed with a draped metal mesh curtain, which glitters and both displays and obscures the bright colors and activity beyond.

Bottom: The cafeteria opens onto Japanese gardens and waterfalls. Its location is ideal as a venue for celebrating community spirit, providing a decompression outlet for staff, indulging in the playful aspects of the corporate culture, and experiencing the blending of indoor and outdoor space.

The **‹kpe›** business plan is a simple one: **partner with other new** media and entertainment **companies to build** digital businesses **and develop** Web potential.

The design of the company's New York City headquarters, not so simple. The 11,000-square-foot (1,022-square-meter) space overlooking Union Square was once an industrial loft. ‹kpe› wanted an office that could accommodate multiple programming needs while allowing for rapid expansion. Various departments, such as business development, finance, marketing, network services, production, and programming needed to be organized in an L-shaped space that offered extremes of light and darkness along a south-facing edge and narrow, extended interior.

Veteran e-design firm Anderson Architects was hired to do the job. With the help of design colleague MJ Sagan and associate Todd Stodolski, principal Ross Anderson quickly responded with a plan that centers around a set of boxes, inspired by the nearby stalls of the Union Square farmer's market, within an overall container. A sturdy yet refined palette of materials modulates spatial relationship and light. The boxes, as Anderson points out, control the mess and enhance the cohesiveness of the space.

Box number one, met directly off the elevator, is dim and clad in galvanized sheet metal; the local company Modelsmith handled all custom metalwork throughout the project. The design of this box is in direct contrast to the rest of the space, which is all about transparency, reflectivity, and light. This initial experience is one that is supposed to be disorienting. It is the "pause button," as Anderson likes to point out, that allows visitors to figure out that they are somewhere else. This area opens up to reception through an overscaled, pivoting plane of blackened steel and cast glass. A gate, in tandem with other high-tech security systems, controls access into the main office for protection. Since most of the employees work twenty-four hours a day, seven days a week, the gate closes at night for protection. Beyond the gate, the space opens to a full wall of

⊗ Top: Upon entering ‹kpe›, visitors are met with a box clad with galvanized sheet metal and a door of blackened steel and cast glass. It opens onto the reception area and waiting room.

⊗ Bottom: Behind the reception area, the space opens to accommodate more public seating. A wall of south-facing, operable windows filters the sun.

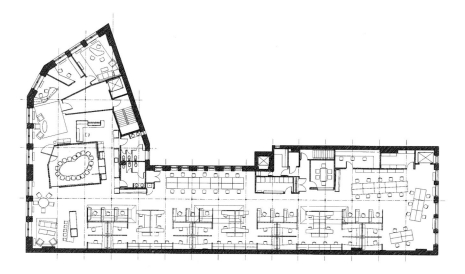

⊗ The 11,000-square-foot open loft office utilizes a long, narrow, L-shaped space in order to allow natural light to saturate all locations.

south-facing, operable windows overlooking Union Square and downtown Manhattan. At night, the windows allow the office to be visible from the outside as a glowing chamber.

Although there was no major structural work to be done on the space, much attention was paid to organizing the shell, and in particular refinishing the wood floors and skim-coating walls and ceilings. Post-renovation, the HVAC playfully weaves through the space as opposed to its clunky and awkward beginnings. New skylights were brought in to replace old, dismal-looking ones and the frames were painted a warm yellow to contrast the predominantly deep colors found in the rest of the space. Another box, a maple plywood storage closet, occupies this open, light-filled environment.

At the end of the reception area, the only full-height walls in the space separate a conference room box clad in cementitious panels. The room contains a free-form table made of a 1 3/4-inch-thick (1.9-centimeter) slab of sandblasted acrylic and metal legs. At the far end of the table is a recessed niche to accommodate laptop computers. Anderson likes to joke that fifteen years ago, such a detail would be used as an ashtray. ICF's plank chairs surround the table as does high-tech audio/visual equipment embedded along the northern wall. The entire south wall of the room is made of dark mirror-glazed panels that pivot and slide, controlling entry into the space, filtering in sun, and reflecting images of passersby. Beyond the conference room are two more boxes—a large-screen television/media center and an aquarium full of small sharks and a fierce eel.

The workstation area was treated as a flexible system in order to meet the company's constant growth needs. ‹kpe› was actually expanding as the design scheme took shape. The architects, in collaboration with Shoufany Custom Woodworking, designed clusters of workstations to sit eighty people with intermediate zones that can be used in a variety of ways. The stations are fabricated of light-gauge steel studs and channel with attached sheets of translucent plastic and fiberglass. Set within the workstation walls are vertically mounted fluorescent lights that illuminate multiple stations. Cast-resin work surfaces resist wear and tear and the back wall was painted a "sick green" to reflect light along the interior spaces. In order for everyone to feel comfortable with his or her personal workspace, the architects offered different forms of compensation. For example, offices near windows have less defined enclosures while those lacking daylight are offered greater privacy.

The intermediate zones can be utilized for different purposes, as the company's needs change. An aluminum cable tray, suspended from the ceiling, carries computer lines as well as overhead fluorescent lights. The double-sided media cabinet in the conference room pierces the back wall to hold equipment in the mailroom and pantry areas. This practical, multi-tasking strategy is well suited to the client's business and proves the design team integrated its approach with the logic and look of the digital world.

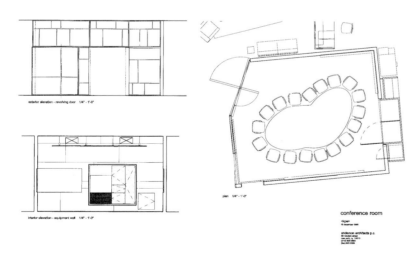

Top: The conference room opens along pivoting and sliding planes of sealed aluminum and tinted, reflective glass.

Bottom: The plans for the conference room include an exterior elevation of the revolving door and an interior elevation of the audio/visual equipment wall. The table and chairs can accommodate up to eighteen people.

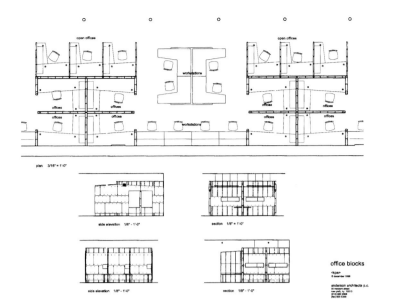

plan 3/16" = 1'-0"

side elevation 1/8" - 1'-0"

section 1/8" - 1'-0"

side elevation 1/8" - 1'-0"

section 1/8" - 1'-0"

office blocks
<kpa>
15 december 1998

anderson architects p.c.
50 wooster street
new york, ny 10013
(212) 420-0369
(fax) 925 5369

⊘ Above Left: In collaboration with Shoufany Custom Woodworking, the architects designed office blocks, clusters of open and more private workstations.

⊘ Above Right: Each workstation includes light-gauge steel with sheets of translucent plastic and fiberglass and cast-resin work surfaces.

⊘ Ross Anderson designed the workstations in clusters with open areas between to accommodate various company objectives.

Clusters of loosely defined offices mark out work areas for various departments.

Those employees lacking direct access to daylight at their workstations were given more private offices.

Hovering **two stories above** New York's Broadway is **a buzzing nexus of concepts** in space and design. Surveying the landscape of **Liquid Design Group** from above,

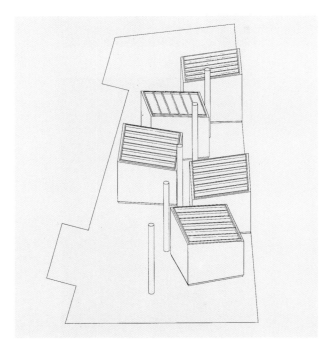

⊗ Top: Freecell's freestanding rooms are equipped with a simple desk and sofa or bed—for late night working—and stand on a red OSB floor.

⊗ Bottom: A line drawing of the stacked, freestanding work rooms.

one observes the light generated from within a series of cubes, dissipating through translucent ceilings. Within one of these private pods, someone's favorite song blends with the reassuring clicks, beeps, and whirs of a computerized command center. Animate shapes glide across the expanse of floor, navigating the currents by five large glowing cubes. The cubes are like gemstones, scattered on alizarin crimson velvet. The room looks like a cargo bay in a science fiction movie. In reality, five people share a workspace here, a collective space which allows each to maintain a degree of individuality. Just a typical day and night in the life of those who work practically 24 hours-a-day at the computer animation company with high-profile clients such as Sony, Pepsi, and Visa.

Liquid Design Group was founded three years ago by Syracuse University graduates and pals Jeff Linnell and Colin Ochel. When it was time to create a 3,500-square-foot (325-square-meter) space with a $28,000 budget, they called on another group of friends, the bi-coastal design collaborative Freecell. John Hartman, Ana Henton, and Troy Ostrander, the Freecell trio, had completed the New York offices of *Tricycle: The Buddhist Review* and several residential projects. Here, the challenge was to divide a trapezoidal space that could accommodate 8 to 15 people, client and in-house meetings, and employee downtime. The client wanted to create a convivial atmosphere that would simultaneously energize and contain the flow of its bust space. With the aid of contractor Scot Webb, the result is bold, utterly contemporary, and fits the client's personality.

The rooms are freestanding, sharing no walls. Each is equipped with a simple desk and sofa or bed for late night working (and there is a bathroom with a shower). They stand on a red floor made of extremely cheap and durable construction-grade oriented strand board (OSB). The 12-foot-by-12-foot (4-meter-by-4-meter) drywall cubes are placed on the red according to the designers' and the client's deliberations over a maquette with movable pieces. The residual space between the rooms is freedom, constantly redefined by transient objects, coursing with activity. For example, the space becomes a presentation room, with a conference table and audio/visual equipment. None of the doors face each other and the rooms have no windows, as dictated by the company's main pursuits. This also addressed privacy issues, but not the need for light. The roofs of individual rooms, therefore, tilt towards the natural light sources on either side of the entire space like sunflowers. Soft light filters through a translucent ceiling made of crysalite, a greenhouse material. Offices are situated along the windowed east wall; on the windowed west end sits a kitchen/dining area and pool table.

The boldly differentiated colors of the installation make an immediate visual impact. However, the initial view is quickly overtaken by one's impression of the scale and shape of the space, which are without doubt the installation's defining qualities. Skewed by heights of 7 ½ (2-meter), 9 (3-meter), and 10 ½ (3.5-meter) feet, the boxes distort one's perception of scale. Depending on the angle of approach, each box can either loom imposingly or taper subtly into the expanse of the room. Their shapes are intimate and otherworldly. In the photographs, they look alternatively miniature and vast, monumental and playful.

Freecell was able to capture Liquid Design Group's sensibilities in the space and all for a mere $8 per square foot. This financial efficiency is couple with innovation: "We imaginatively accommodated the exacting needs of the occupant," say the designers, "forging from limited resources not only a unique space but a novel idea, a 24-hour-a-day refuge for employees and freelancers."

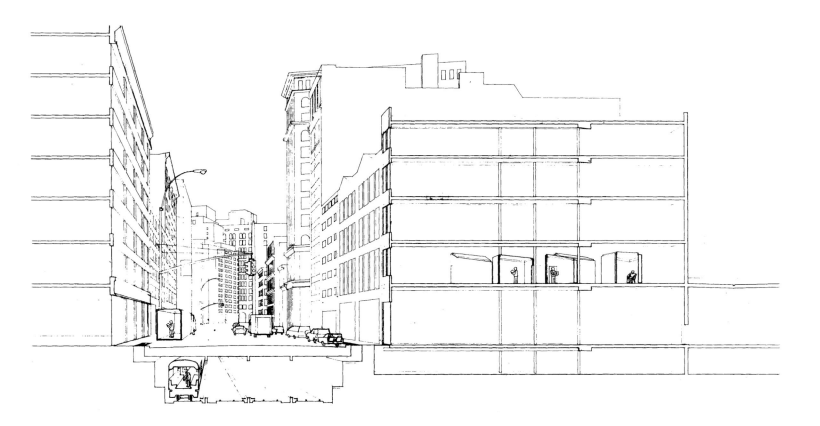

⊘ Top: The 12-foot-by-12-foot (4-meter-by-4-meter) drywall cubes are placed according to the designers' and the client's deliberations over a maquette with movable pieces.

⊘ Bottom: Seen in the context of the local cityscape, the architects' drawing of Liquid Design group's office space.

New Zealander Grant Mitchell came to **England from Auckland** fifteen years ago as a trained computer graphic designer. After a series of **various jobs** with Imagination and Pentagram, Mitchell **teamed up with former classmates**

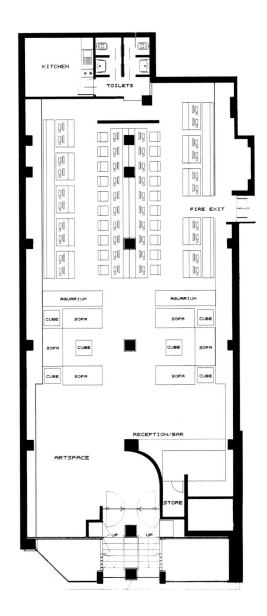

George and Toula Philippakos, tech whizzes, and art director Alistair Kay to join the ranks of young cyber entrepreneurs. They opened the Internet café Nutopia in London's Covent Garden. The cyber-lounge, designed by the team now called Nucreatives, draws it inspiration directly from a statement made by John Lennon and Yoko Ono in 1973: "We announce the birth of a conceptual country, Nutopia. It has no land, boundaries, or passports, only people." Also thrown in the design mix, sleek, streamlined, and ultra-cool images from Stanley Kubrick's *2001: A Space Odyssey* and *Star Wars'* director George Lucas' first film *THX- 1138*.

More than a cyber café, Nutopia is a public office for corporate groups and individuals as well as firms with a nomadic workforce to access a bank of forty flat-screen, low radiation monitors for joint work sessions. The Computer Zone, which houses the rows of hybrid iMac computers, has front ends that are PC-based systems powered by Intel Pentium chips. Note that all of the computers face inwards, away from the wall, to encourage interaction. Nucreative's initial brief, to "build an environment that gives the impression of floating through space," was achieved by creating an-other-worldly, high-gloss facility that embraces technology and presents it in a calming, stress-free environment. Large fish tanks separate the workspaces from the lounge (and are said to de-ionize the air); the lounge is furnished with simple, contemporary sofas designed by Mitchell and Philippe Starck's La Marie chairs as well as custom light tables. The space includes airy, aquamarine lighting that is diffused through translucent PVC walls bouncing off glass divider screens and a shiny, white, epoxy resin floor. This creates a soft, ambient light and the illusion of being submerged underwater. Walls are backlit white rubber stretched over fluorescent tubes gelled turquoise.

◈ Nucreatives' floor plans for the Internet café.

◈ The Computer Zone houses rows of hybrid iMacs that have PC-based front ends powered by Intel Pentium chips.

⊗ Large fish tanks separate the
⊗ workspaces from the lounge
and de-ionize the air.

The space also functions as a gallery and juice bar/café. An area simply referred to as Launchpad is a platform for artists and designers using new technology. The original display includes Paul Friedlander's Lightwaves, whirling dervishes of colored light spinning toward the ceiling; *Four Seven Three*, an interactive wall panel that dims and brightens as people pass designed by Jason Brugesn; and Wave, an aluminum sofa by star St. Martin's graduate Ansel Thompson that incorporates fiber optics running through it. Also on show, Friedlander's *Dark Matter,* a sculpture that shines chromastrobic light along the length of three rapidly gyrating skipping ropes that give rise to three oscillating vertical columns of textured light. A hidden computer continuously redefines the form and color of these columns. Visitors can also interact with *Dark Matter* by using two high-frequency sound beams to alter the speed of the rope's vibrations and the light colors. For example, a visitor can place his or her body through the beams and cause a disturbance that is fed back to the motor driving the rope into the chromastrobe to illuminate the sculpture.

Here, technology meets creativity in an environment designed to appeal to the style conscious. Nutopia's future? Grandiose. Facilities worldwide equipped with an interactive, online database for computer artists and people working in new media (or any hot-tech industry) and exhibition spaces showcasing the latest in robot technology.

⊘ Technology and nature blend in this space.

⊘ The lounge is furnished with simple, contemporary sofas designed by Mitchell and Philippe Starck's La Marie chairs as well as custom light tables.

The Launchpad space functions as a gallery, an area that is a platform for artists and designers using new technology.

The New York City firm The Phillips Group combined forces with Richard Fernau and Laura Hartman, principals at Fernau & Hartman of San Francisco, **to create the 85,000-square-foot** (7,897-square-meter) **office and studio production** space of

Oxygen Media in Chelsea Markets at 75 Ninth Avenue, New York City. Oxygen, a media company catering to women, is forging ahead with the combined force of cable network television and the Internet. Oxygen's manifesto states that "like the chemical element itself, Oxygen will seek combinations everywhere."

The headquarters, which also serves as the set for Oxygen's cable channel, aided by a floating blimp with remote control, was designed as a dynamic, egalitarian office that would allow a start-up, dot-com company the greatest flexibility to organize itself in varying ways around an evolving set of tasks. With a limited budget of approximately $60 per square foot, the overall design accommodates a variety of office types, ranging from open to closed. However, the majority of employees work at open stations. Being in the open allows staff to enjoy the light, space, and air that attracted Oxygen to the two-story, loft-like space of this former Nabisco cookie factory.

Like new media companies, architects combine strengths. Design architects Richard Fernau and project architect David Kau, along with Aaron Thorton, Michael Roche, Tom Powers, Fred Dust, Jason Bell, and Aleks Baharlo, built movement into the design, as The Phillips Group produced a flexible oxygen filled workspace. Visitors are first greeted by a serene and simple entrance followed by a reception area, with a custom-designed desk, Bright Mia series furniture, and a custom bubble tank.

For the rest of the space, features of versatility abound in the converted factory. Structures with names such as the Tower, Gull Wings, the Quilt, the Butterfly, and the Zippers were originally created with digital renderings. The industrial workstations are flexible modules, aptly named Metal Zippers and Wood Zippers, which slide back and forth for optimum adjustments and quick reconfiguration, and they form the backbone of the design. As linear elements, they carry out only the required services, including wiring and cabling, throughout the space, but they also house individual and company-wide storage. In contrast to the wooden zipper—a handcrafted wood stud

⊘ Virtual architectural rendering
⊘ and floor plan for Oxygen's new
⊘ Chelsea Market offices.

wall—the metal zipper is prefabricated from Equipto's industrial pallet racks (typically found in car repair shops) and finished with custom millwork. To this modular system, the designers added infrastructure cable trays, docklight tasklighting, and storage "suitcases." In-line skate wheels attach to the tracks on the shelves, allowing the desks to slide together and become larger, conference tables for impromptu meetings. In addition, they experimented with Butterflies, acoustic privacy screens from KnollTextiles that slide along standard barn door hardware, and overhead acoustic "Gull Wings" that rotate and pivot to define temporary collaborative areas. The Tower, a thirty-five-foot (10.7-meter) wood structure penetrating up from the seventh floor through the eighth floor, provides conference and studio production space. The Quilt, a series of panels with exposed fasteners, also connects two 20,000-square-foot (1,858-square-meter)floors and can be seen from the 1,200-square-foot (111.5-square-meter) mezzanine across the vast space.

Essential to this open-office environment are an unusually high number of idiosyncratic open and closed conference areas. Each varies greatly, as defined by privacy, access, and acoustics. Several conference rooms of different sizes are clustered around a central light well cut between floors. While the Zippers organize the space laterally, the light well orchestrates movement through the space vertically. The entrance is on the lower floor with a main stair leading upward to a vaulted clerestory space equipped with operable windows. At any given moment, the light well is a venue for a dozen informal conversations. Together, the light well, zipper, and conference rooms create a new symbolic focal point—a forty-foot (12.2-meter) canyon filled with the energy of a new start-up.

⊗ The overall design accommodates a variety of office types, ranging from open to closed. However, the majority of employees work at open stations.

⊗ A serene and simple entrance soon gives way to a reception area, with a custom-designed desk, Bright Mia series furniture, and a custom bubble tank.

⊗ The metal zipper workstations are prefabricated from industrial pallet racks typically found in car repair shops and finished with custom millwork.

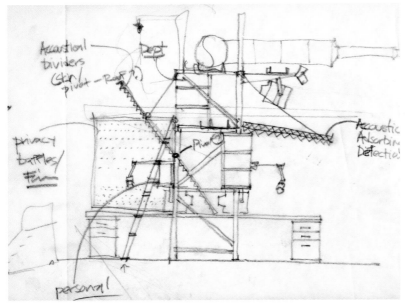

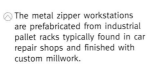

⊗ The metal zipper workstations are prefabricated from industrial pallet racks typically found in car repair shops and finished with custom millwork.

⊗ The designers experimented with Butterflies, acoustic privacy screens that slide along standard barn door hardware, and overhead acoustic "Gull Wings" that rotate and pivot to define temporary collaborative areas.

⊗ Model of the Oxygen workstations.

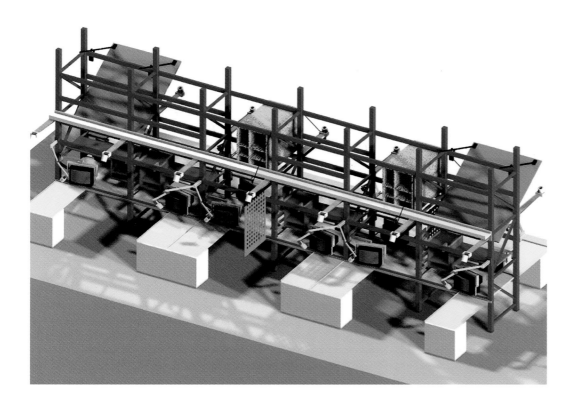

The Tower, a thirty-five-foot (10.7-meter) wood structure penetrating up from the seventh floor through the eighth floor, provides conference and studio production space.

The space includes an unusually high number of idiosyncratic open and closed conference areas. Each varies greatly, as defined by privacy, access, and acoustics. Several conference rooms of different sizes are clustered around a central light well cut between floors.

Once upon a time, **Pomegranit,** a company that specializes in the postproduction and editing of **high-end national** television commercials for leading national advertising agencies worldwide, had its offices in **San Francisco's "advertising gulch"**

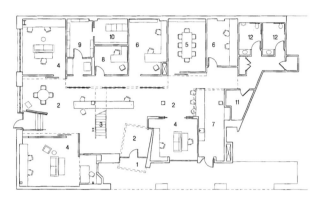

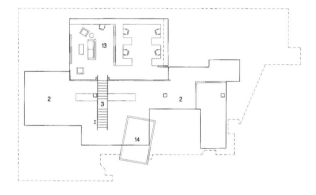

⊘ Floor plans of Pomegranit's new 6,000 square-foot offices.

⊘ The reception area in the Great Hall is a simple and elegant introduction to the company's more hectic business.

on the top floor of a landmark brick warehouse that characterizes the city's legendary Barbary Coast waterfront. With expansive views of the San Francisco Bay and Bay Bridge, life seemed good for the employer and employees. But soon a landlord/tenant issue required the company to move into a two-level, 6,000-square-foot (557-square-meter) space at the building's base. Holey Associates was charged with the task of creating new digs and convincing staff that the move down was a good one. Principal John Holey found himself with a tough sell.

Holey was faced with a few requirements. Since the process of editing advertising commercials is highly collaborative and involves many meetings with both the agency and the agency's high profile clients, it was important that the new facility have an open environment that affords a range of spaces for collaborative work. The designer also had to provide varying levels of privacy as well as editing suites, a private conference room, dining area, and private workspace.

The new site, once an office for Saatchi & Saatchi, was grim, with suspended ceilings, fluorescent lighting, and a traditional plan—private offices at the perimeter and daylight-lacking cubicles clustered in the core. There was one asset—a potentially interesting mezzanine space. After interior demolition, an open space with twenty-five-foot-high (7.6-meter) ceilings supported by redwood rafters appeared. To integrate the mezzanine, Holey and his team installed a direct-access stairway with woven steel mesh guardrails by the Howard Wire Cloth Company as well as maple treads and visers. All flooring is simply sandblasted and steel concrete. To bring in daylight, he replaced part of the entry's elevation with frameless glass panels. Then the two twenty-foot-wide (6.1-meter) bricked-in archways were replaced with doors and windows leading to a cobblestone alley. Large glass doors allow Pomegranit's creative activity to be seen from the street, as well as bring light into the space.

From the kitchen, the view of Great Hall includes the concrete-slab reception desk that wraps around a supporting column.

Pomegranit's grand exterior, which opens up to a cobblestone alley, lets passersby sneak a peak at the creative team. An expansive twenty-foot-wide (6.1-meter) window replaced the existing brick section within the building's arch.

Typically, a client will arrive to the office, talk about the project, and then move to the editing suites. These suites function as both lounges and high-tech workrooms. Holey, with the help of his design team, including Carl Bridgers, Joan Diengott, Edie Chaska, David Seidel, Greg Keffer, and Patrick Booth, as well as the contractor Plant Construction Company, had to accommodate twelve people, including Pomegranit's four principals, two of whom use the editing suites as executive offices.

In the center of the office of the Great Hall, an open, industrial-looking expanse forms the focal point of the workspace. Included here are the reception area, an informal area for conversation, and a snack bar. A reception desk made out of concrete slab that wraps around a timber column and is supported by ceiling-hung steel cables dominates the space. A Herman Miller Aeron chair finishes it off. A transparent, enclosed editing suite is convenient for visiting clients and allows for audio privacy. Four colors, three shades of each, were used to distinguish each editing suite. The strongest application of each tone is expressed at doorways through integrally colored plaster mixed with marble dust. Harking back to shoji screens, sliding panels behind the reception desk consist of a double layer of scalloped acrylic sheets in a maple frame. These translucent mobile planes provide privacy for the video library and offices located in a block below the mezzanine.

The Great Hall functions much like "home office," as Holey describes it with amenities more often found in the home. The kitchen and lunch table promote staff interaction; open computer terminals and Sony Play Station encourages clients to bring children along. Amenities like these particularly suit the needs of a creative business with a comfortable work process. The informal conversation area, with a sofa grouped around a table and an Eames plywood chair, is used for collaborative meetings of various groups, individuals taking a break from the hectic pace of work, or visiting clients. To further soften the industrial-style space, Holey chose vintage elements—English pine pocket doors and a chandelier, for example—and continues to present homelike references.

The project, completed in eight months for approximately $55 per square feet, reflects a visual image of creativity in the advertising community. And, the benefit for Holey Associates? "We've gotten work," says Holey, "by taking people through and having the client rave."

Top: The view of the Great Hall and color-coded editing suite with lounge furniture. Each editing room measures approximately 250 to 350 square feet (23.23 to 32.52 square meters).

Bottom: A view through the Great Hall to the editing suite and mezzanine level, one of the more distinguishing features in the new office.

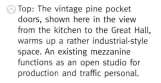 Top: The vintage pine pocket doors, shown here in the view from the kitchen to the Great Hall, warms up a rather industrial-style space. An existing mezzanine functions as an open studio for production and traffic personal.

Bottom Left: From behind the moveable screen, one of four color-coded editing suites can be seen.

Bottom Right: A staff member demonstrates the translucency of the moveable screen that hides a video library and editing suite.

The new home of **Predictive Systems Inc.,** a fast-growing consultancy start-up that develops global networks and Internet-related services, is in New York's midtown area, specifically **38th Street and 5th Avenue.**

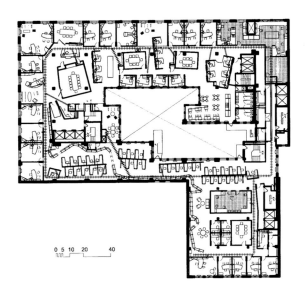

According to company president and co-founder Robert Belau, the concept for the latest office space had to deal with flexibility, image, and growth/expansion as critical requirements. Recently, the firm grew from a staff of twelve occupying 3,500 square feet (325 square meters) in a downtown Tribeca warehouse to one hundred fifteen employees in need of some breathing room.

For the design team at Anderson Architects, the New York-based firm that handled the project as well as the client's first warehouse office, creating an open space for staff members, conference rooms, private offices, and support facilities, had few constraints. The new site was similar to the old, and the team, including vice president MJ Sagan and project architect Caroline Otto, wanted to maintain a downtown feel in an uptown world. An open concrete shell, the new penthouse space had generous light that filled up 22,000 square feet (2,044 square meters). The main challenge came from the floor plate's "notched, distorted" configuration, explains Anderson. "But it guaranteed built-in parcels of territory as an antidote to workstation overload."

The scheme required a mix of open and private accommodations plus the typical support systems for executives, marketing, and human resources department. Also, the offices would be home base for the firm's New York consultants, who spend most of their time off-site. Up to as much as 80 percent of Predictive employees can be out of the office at any given time, so the space had to appeal to everyone constantly coming and going throughout the day.

A double-faced, steel-framed construction, nicknamed "the chromosome" by Anderson, moves through the space. There are steel wire storage components for personal belongings and bright orange Vitra mobile carts fitted with laptops, cell phones, and other needed peripherals. Employees can wheel these carts up to an available workstation, plug in, and get to work. Whiteboards and integrated lighting systems complete "the chromosome."

⊘ Predictive Systems' 3,500 square-foot floor plan.

⊘ Bright orange Vitra mobile carts are fitted with laptops, cell phones, and other needed peripherals for employees who need flexible work areas.

Anderson insisted upon "maintaining the visual connection between departments as well as providing natural light for everyone. To achieve these goals, Anderson wiped out five-foot-high (1.5-meter) panel enclosures and separated work units, which are both custom designed and Unifor systems, with cork panels that rise just above eye level. He punched through adjacent walls with a series of boxes made of translucent green acrylic and left most of the ceiling plane open to the slab. Suspended from the thirteen-and-a-half-foot-high (4.1-meter) ceiling are wings of perforated metal, Sheetrock or Tectum panels that define specific areas without obstructing light.

Private offices are fronted with panels of the same translucent green acrylic. For conference rooms, translucency is achieved through pivoting doors with aluminum frames anchoring fiberglass panels. Off the reception area, the primary conference room connects with its surroundings in a most unusual way: a 1,000-gallon fish tank from the House of Fins with a coral reef and indigenous ecosystem pierces the dividing wall that is similar to the acrylic boxes and filters light and sound.

Most of the furnishings are custom designed. Most desktops, especially in private offices, are aluminum-edged laminate. Private areas also have Anderson-designed library units made of cement board panels anchoring aluminum shelves and maple storage components. The reception desk is made of cement-board panels combined with one-inch-thick (3-centimeter) sandblasted acrylic slabs; the conference table, from Modelsmith, has a sandblasted acrylic top supported by aluminum legs. Rugs are also custom made through Sherland & Ferrington; their color-block graphics can be found in informal meeting areas as well as the large open office area. The cafeteria, which seats approximately thirty-five people, is simply defined by a freestanding, stained plywood partition framing stainless steel appliances.

The project was designed in four months and built in fourteen weeks, and Anderson and Belau are both happy with the results. Anderson continues to enjoy wandering in the space and watching how all of the pieces fit together, while Belau appreciates the downtown feel of the uptown space that combines functionality with high-tech creativity.

Work areas, which are both custom designed and Unifor systems, are separated with cork panels that rise just above eye level.

Predictive's private offices are fronted with panels of the same translucent green acrylic.

A 1,000-gallon fish tank that sits on a rusted steel stand connects the reception and conference areas. The conference room has an aluminum and fiberglass-pivoting door.

The cafeteria sits approximately thirty-five and is defined by a freestanding, stained plywood partition framing stainless-steel appliances.

STUDIOS, led by Kevin Estrada and John Henderson, began working with the **RiskMetrics Group** as they started a real-estate search **for their first offices in downtown Manhattan.** The RiskMetrics Group, **a recently established spin-off of**

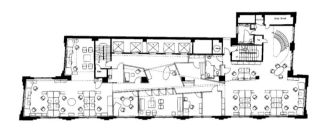

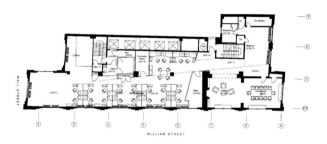

⊘ Partial floor plans for the 18,000-square-foot, three-floor offices of RiskMetrics Group.

the J.P. Morgan financial service empire that is in the business of risk analysis and developing software technology to identify and manage financial risk, wanted an open, modern space where it could build an office culture of easy communication and high energy. After looking at several properties, the company finally settled on offices—all 18,000 square feet (1,672 square meters)—on the top three floors of a prewar building on New York's Wall Street that could accommodate seventy-six employees. The design scheme is a simple one: direct aesthetic opposition to its more conservative parent company. How else can a company ensure an ample pool of talented employees in a market where groovy digs is now the norm?

In spite of that mandate, the formal, sweeping staircase and wood paneled library/conference room were saved from demolition, as each quickly recalled a bygone era of Wall Street banking and were reflections of the financial worlds of old and new. The existing ceilings in the library and conference rooms were removed and the exposed concrete structure painted black. A retractable video scrim, by John Creech Productions, is used for projections and to separate the library and conference rooms. A custom-designed coffee table, by Kevin Estrada, contains cast-rubber pieces and provides a quirky respite from the traditional surrounding materials and products. The series of wood-paneled rooms and an old kitchen were left as found, though their purpose has not yet been discovered.

In contrast, the remainder of the space was conceived as an expression of the future of Wall Street and investment technology. Planned as an open environment for software writers and developers, there are just two private offices and enclosed spaces for holding private meetings. The entrance level has a central core with open-plan wings to the east and west. Sight lines were established between the two wings of the office to further connect the diverse activities of the company. Between the Web and data area to the west and the administrative and sales area to the east is the reception zone, as well as a conference room, support functions, and two private offices. Sandwiched between the two private offices, which are enclosed behind translucent walls, the conference room is hidden by an acrylic and aluminum wall constructed by South Hudson Glass & Metal. The room has south-facing windows that fill the reception area directly to the north with natural light.

A retractable video scrim divides the library from the conference room and is used for projections.

Wherever possible, dropped ceilings were removed to expose the building's concrete and plaster structure, exposing the window openings in their greatest dimension to flood the space with natural light. Those walls and ceilings required for the few enclosed rooms to be placed at unexpected angles to one another, sculpting the space and revealing dramatic views across and between the floors. The resulting effect is one modernity with an abundance of clean open space and light to create an uplifting work environment for this young, growing business.

One floor above is a large open workspace for programmers, the library, and conference room. A double-height space formerly held another staircase, which was removed to filter light into work areas. Traditional workstations were abandoned in favor of seven-foot-

wide desks from the European manufacturer Vitra, making for expansive workstations that can accommodate the large computer monitors used by employees. Programmers sit at open desks with maple-veneer work surfaces and bright blue compartments for CPU equipment.

Despite the long-standing traditions of the RiskMetrics Group's parent company, CEO Ethan Berman wanted a space that was uplifting and fashionable. To that extent, the offices are also enlivened by artwork; a revolving exhibition of contemporary art is installed throughout the space, with curatorial services provided by Kevin Estrada and Berman himself. With a combination of art and commerce, RiskMetrics Group created an environment that serves its needs well.

⊗ Despite the need for a modern office interior, the designers kept the existing wood paneling in the upper floor conference room and library. The coffee table was designed by Kevin Estrada of STUDIOS.

The reception area, decked out with Vitra furniture, opens onto a conference room, which is furnished with Herman Miller chairs and benches.

Programmers work at Vitra stations with maple-veneer work surfaces and bright blue compartments for CPU equipment.

William Green, the design giant behind the **Scient** company's New York office, describes his **finished work as "classically inspired contemporary interiors."**

Pop artist Andy Warhol's former office became Scient's main conference room. The wall paneling is of pecan wood.

Scient's New York office occupies 37,500 square feet on three floors.

Not typical of an e-commerce business. But, there's nothing typical about this client or the designer. Green's repertoire consists of varied commercial jobs for world-famous clients here and abroad as well as residential interiors/house constructions in New York, California, and Thailand.

Founded in October 1997 and operative four months later, the San Francisco-based Scient officially hired Green, and his design team Yukari Watanabe, Tony Klein, and Valery Nitikin, after he won the competitive design commission in April 1999. The job, which took six months from design conception to move-in time, cost $40 per square foot for construction.

Wanting to open its first East Coast office as expected in Manhattan, the company could not predict the curious location—pop artist Andy Warhol's former factory on Broadway at Union Square. It provides 37,500 square feet (3,484 square meters) equally divided on three floors. Staff count comes to about two hundred forty, excluding the company's clients, who often participate in projects in the last two or more months of the development time.

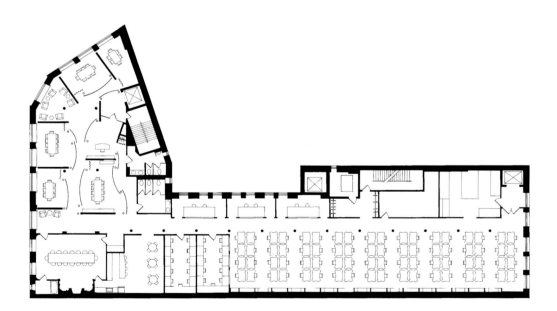

The design of the third floor, where most of the collaborative work takes place, began with a thorough clean-out. Unfortunately, excavating the ex-Warholian work/playground did not uncover any fortuitous finds of Mao or Marilyn silk-screen mementos. Still, there was a nice surprise—a fully wood-paneled room with a stone mantel fireplace, formerly the artist's own office and now Scient's largest conference room. There are six such gathering spaces on the third floor, supplemented with informal get-together spots and forming, along with a sizeable reception area, the public zone. The long horizontal stretch of the L-shaped footprint is devoted to in-house work operations.

Within the public sector, conference and lounge areas are separated by partition walls set perpendicularly to the perimeter and allow maximum inflow of unblocked daylight. Reception room-facing fronts are screened by shaped transparent panels with bent-wood slats, sometimes curtained and, as when the entire zone is used for business entertainment, left open. Near the elevator entry, the paneling process is repeated and amplified with ticker-tape-type logo letters. Extant flooring in the waiting area was covered with 8 ½ in. x 5 ½ in. (22 cm x 14 cm) bits of off-white paper, then covered with layers of polyurethane. Further emphasizing the public sector's character are hung ceilings, shaving three feet (0.9 meters) from the elsewhere prevailing fourteen-foot (4.3-meter) height.

Top and Right: The waiting area with bowed entries to the conference room. Confetti flooring is made of polyurethane-sealed paper on wood.

Bottom: Scient logos appear at the meeting-room entry in the elevator vestibule.

The wide open band housing project designers/developers' workstations keep mobility and flexibility in mind. Constant regrouping is (as anyone having anything to do with new media knows) a way of life for all colleagues. (At Scient, the staff is referred to as colleagues, not employees.) Doing most of their work on laptops, they need correctly-sized countertops for easiest access to equipment and papers. Even more important is quick transference from one place to another on short notice, without cluttering the vacated slot with a mess of unplugged wires. Therefore, custom-sized desks are set on casters and provided with cabling that connects to overhead ladder trays. Green's briefing material refers to freestanding workstations "connected to their electronic data communications infrastructure via a vertical connector from the top to the bundle of wiring options existing at the 'techno' ceiling plane". Green also speaks of "technology woven into design," reiterating that when

there's movement, the wiring goes with the desk rather than being left dangling from trays on high.

Contrasts in finishes provide design details. Custom desks are of maple and plastic laminates; wall panels at the corridor under the ladder tray are dark-stained reconstituted wood interspersed with vinyl-stripped doors (a surfacing more commonly used to insulate refrigerated rooms). Forming checkerboard-like patterns are storage lockers of clear maple with black laminate, designed by Green and concealing items behind doors or in drawers.

Subsequently, designing the fourth and fifth floors was easier and faster for the design team, and within months of the first expansion step, Scient went global and opened fourteen outposts worldwide. There goes the neighborhood.

The wiring for Green's custom-designed workstations is connected to the overhead electronic data communications infrastructure. The far side of the corridor alternates stained reconstituted wood with vinyl-strip doors.

Following the TBWA/Chiat/Day merger six years ago, adman Jay Chiat has **returned to business as chairman of** Screaming Media, an Internet information resource or, **in other words,**

an Internet content provider. Setting up shop in the landmark Starrett Lehigh building in the far West corner of New York City's Chelsea district, the 25,000-square-foot (2,323-square-meter) space is an experiment in creating an open, non-hierarchical workplace. A space that allows a permanent place for each of the one hundred sixty employees, whose average age is twenty-six, and is also architecturally distinctive with a sense of energy, excitement, and community, words that easily describe the company's work ethic and vibe as well as the founder's notions of "new business." Remember Chiat's well-documented foray into hoteling a few years back?

Ceramicist, artist, and architect Jane Sachs and partner/architect Thomas Hut of Hut Sachs Studio, along with project architect Lawrence McDonald, were hired on the basis of previous work with a multitude of new media clients and a long list of impressive residential work. With a $700,000 budget and a five-month deadline, the team quickly decided to disregard the "dumpy" design of Screaming Media's previous offices at 55 Wall Street, in the heart of the city's financial district. They wanted to depart from traditional notions of rigid office space, preferring instead to envelop its occupants in "dynamically folding spaces," says both Sachs and Hut. "No doors; no corner offices; no cubicles. Rather a smooth and at times striated web of technology and color". The results seem at once reminiscent of both sculptor Richard Serra's Torqued Ellipses and Frank Gehry's spatial manipulations but with a clear language all its own. Employees have described it as "a surreal den of crazy colors, mind-bending shapes, and conga-beating energy"—a Screaming Media salesperson ritually drums on congas to welcome another subscriber into their global content network.

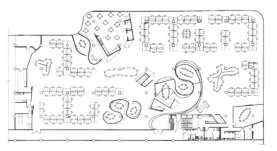

⊗ Top: Central to the space is a Masonite volume; seen here, the first of three meeting rooms immediately beyond the reception area.

⊗ Bottom: Screaming Media's 25,000-square-foot (2,323-square-meter) space, plus an anticipated expansion of 18,000 square feet (1,672 square meters) will accommodate three hundred fifty employees.

⊗ The reception area obscures a full office view; the interior's full scope is discovered as visitors progress. Milton Glaser's graphic work can be seen throughout the space.

⊗ In this case, the ever-present torqued walls hide one of many conference areas.

Working with an unusually large amount of square footage, twelve-foot-high (3.7-meter) ceilings, and panoramic views of New York, New Jersey, and the river in between, Hut and Sachs sculpted volumes of Masonite and tinted plaster to form enclosures for reception, conference rooms, phone areas, and a dining room. The yellow trapezoidal phone booth, remarks one employee, is an oasis for screamers when they need a private moment. Though seeming vague, the floor plan is based around workstations that follow an orthogonal order and relate to a series of right angles, with columns for electrical and data wiring and alternative work places set off the grid.

Having to accommodate new media tools, such as flat screen technology, Hut and Sachs collaborated with the German contract furniture manufacturer Vitra. The plan: customize architects Antonio Citterio's and Glen Oliver Low's already-existing Ad Hoc system to develop Screaming Media's own work stations with one-inch-thick sanded acrylic desktops, metal project boxes, and divider panels made of perforated metal. To ensure ample room for future employee increases and needs, each workstation only measures 5'4" x 3' (1.6 m x 0.9 m). There are also freeform, bright Formica-topped work surfaces, named pond tables, for meetings—both public and private—that break up the monotony of the sea of workstations. A usual stamp of authenticity for Hut, Sachs, and Jay Chiat, all employees have outside views, including the chairman himself, who sits in the middle of a highly trafficked pathway amidst his employees. Also, a bold use of color and graphics to keep both the interior space and employees' energy level high. Among the many wild tones and subdued hues used throughout the space, pale green prevails because, according to the architects and client, studies have shown that this particular color is close to the shade an employee should look at when resting his or her eyes from computer glare. Graphic guru Milton Avery, a long-time friend of Chiat, provides the words and phrases found painted on the surfaces. Words like "spontaneity" and "power" intermingle with "sensitiveness" and "primitive," offering words of wisdom to work by.

Both practical and conceptual issues were on the boards for client and architects, who worked with models in their own offices as well as onsite at the installation for the contractor's benefit. Much of the architectural sculpting was done in the field so both parties could get a true feeling for the shapes, volume, and handling of the offices. Keeping a realistic yet abstract design scheme also proved ingenious. By the end of 2000, Screaming Media projects a population spurt reaching three hundred fifty employees. So, a breakthrough expansion, 18,000 square feet nearby, ready, and waiting, is in the future.

SCREAMING MEDIA **149**

⊘ Since there are few local hang-
outs in the neighborhood the
company set up a café and
lounge for employees.

⊘ Some of Screaming Media's conference area is more open to
public viewing so employees
can share in information.

Above Left: Glaser's words enliven the entryway into the dining and pantry areas.

Above Right: The bold use of color and graphics keeps both the interior space and employees' energy level high.

1 RECEPTION
2 LARGE MEETING ROOM
3 WORK AREA
4 PHONE BOOTH
5 PANTRY
6 POND TABLE
7 WORKSTATIONS
8 WORK ROOM
9 WORKING VIEW

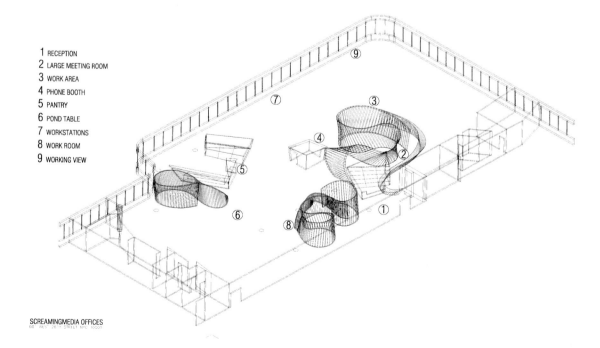

SCREAMINGMEDIA OFFICES
60 WEST 28TH STREET NYC 10001

The New York architecture firm Gerner + Valcarcel had barely begun to handle the 25,000-square-foot (2,323-square-meter) program for **SFX Entertainment** when **the company's corporate agenda changed...dramatically.**

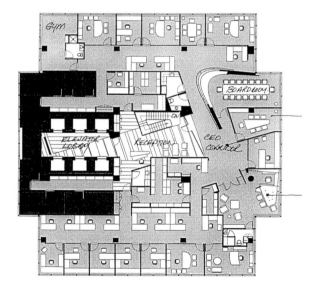

The company's main focus is the entertainment industry, including music, concert promotions, theater, radio, sports, and marketing. Shortly after Gerner + Valcarcel came on board, the radio-directed business was sold and several companies in similar industry fields were purchased. The corporate focus was extended to include the organizing, producing, scheduling, packaging, promoting, and merchandising of live performances involving singers, bands, actors, and sports figures. This shift obviously affected the interior scheme and became the starting point for deliberations between client and designer, in particular partner Richard. As one of the firm's founding partners, Richard has designed more than 2 million square feet of space and knew well how to work with such an ever-changing project.

First and foremost, the client requested that the office design reflect the company's industry and not present a typical image of a corporate headquarters in midtown Manhattan. In other words, stay away from a staid and over-dignified space that supposedly conveyed a mainstream corporation. The company CEO preferred something chic that had visual ties to the world of show business; something with more imagination than the usual audio/visual gimmickry common to entertainment offices. The client got exactly what he ordered: a dynamic space that sets the company apart from the competition.

Private offices, assistant's stations, two gyms, a lunchroom, support areas, and reception desks at each end of the connecting staircase cover two floors in a midtown Madison Avenue building between 59th and 60th Streets. The plan is best described as a series of planes at diverse angles interrupted by the "swoosh" that houses the boardroom and a backlit glass prism that includes the public stair connecting the two floors. In fact, when lit the stairs become a two-story light fixture. The reception desks, created in collaboration with Walter P. Sauer, act as foils to the stair with gentle curves fabricated in, curly maple, and stainless steel, all opaque materials.

An exercise in what calls manipulated, eccentric geometry, the glass beacon enclosing the stairs is placed to one side of the reception zone and is sheathed with ribbed glazing acting like a prism that fractures and animates reflected colors. The shimmering parts seem to change when in reality it is the moving onlooker who visually activates the colorplay. The staircase itself is made of stainless-steel risers and stringers, terrazzo-composite treads, and leather-wrapped exterior railings.

⊗ Top: SFX Entertainment's offices are located on Madison Avenue on two floors high above midtown, with splendid views.

⊗ Bottom: Gerner + Valcarcel handled the 25,000 square-foot renovation process for SFX Entertainment.

⊗ Top: Simple and elegant design, as seen here in the boardroom, is prevalent throughout the space.

⊗ The reception desks work with stair's gentle curves and is fabricated in, curly maple, and stainless steel, all opaque materials.

⊗ The staircase itself is made of stainless-steel risers and stringers, terrazzo-composite treads, and leather-wrapped exterior railings.

On the upper floor, visitors pass through a translucent glass wall into a passageway that accesses the chairman's suite and boardroom, a space that is seen as a collective entity among employees. The boardroom is encased in an amorphous, blue plaster wall with a glass window in it. The lit band of teeth acts as a luminous backdrop for curving, wraparound credenzas under shelving. The structure's outer ledge and railings are, says, articulations of the curve that do not serve a purpose but aid in the fun of the design. The corridor is highlighted by a custom, backlit structure suspended from the ceiling that is fabricated of stainless-steel piping and fabric. The ceiling system's geometry reflects the entire space's geometrics. This forces the perspective to the double iron doors that are the entrance to the chairman's office suite.

In the CEO's domain is a "structure" that vaguely resembles a tapered canopy. It is suspended from the ceiling and runs from the boardroom's curve to the office's double-door entry. Made of polyester fabric put into a wrinkle-crinkling solution and then stretched up to a precalculated point over stainless-steel tubing, corner pieces of the frame are welded and individual fabric cuts are hand-sewn to the metal supports. The piece has an effect of a faintly corrugated silvery-gray sail or cloud floating overhead.

Since the SFX premises are in a side-core building, the relatively long walk from elevator lobby to the CEO's area becomes something of a sightseeing tour. This created an ambience keyed into the client's business. It took roughly nine months to complete the job, aided by managing partner Miguel Valcarcel and team members Dubrovka Antic, Victor Colom, Espen Segal, Tami Wassong, and Christopher Trumble. Also on the job were lighting consultants and MEP engineer Flack and Kurtz as well as construction manager AJ Contracting.

⬙ The geometric curves of the ceiling panel play against the round curves of the conference room walls; the blue punctuates the space.

⬙ The band of lighting acts as a luminous backdrop for curving, wraparound credenzas under shelving.

The corridor is highlighted by a custom, backlit structure suspended from the ceiling that is fabricated of stainless-steel piping and fabric.

The boardroom is encased in an amorphous, blue plaster wall with a glass window in it that looks like a big whale with teeth.

The site: 15,000 square feet (1,394 square meters) in a three-story generic office building in Scottsdale, Arizona. The program: An advertising/design and marketing firm, whose clients include Ford, Coca-Cola, General Mills, and

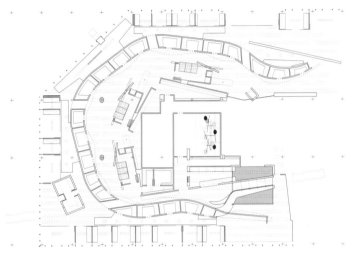

SHR Perceptual Management hired Morphosis to take 15,000 square feet (1,394 square meters) in a three-story generic office building and create a unique architecture that communicated their identity as creative problem solvers.

M&M/Mars, sought a unique architecture that communicated their identity as creative problem solvers in contrast to the homogenous context of the existing Scottsdale environment. The firm: Morphosis, the twenty-five-year-old Santa Monica-based architecture studio lead by principal Thom Mayne, project architect Patrick J. Tighe, and the design team of Saffet Kaya Bekirogru, Ung Joo Scott Lee, David Plotkin, and David Rindlaub. Four key attributes of the client were identified as qualities that were to be expressed through the architecture: strategic discovery, refined precision, genuine partnering, and dynamic impact. Cost: $60 per square foot.

Conflicting needs for privacy and team interaction were identified as alternate systems in juxtaposition. Addressing these issues, the interior defines the different functional zones of a design firm with a set of distinct architectural gestures within a nondescript normative office environment. The existing building core, together with the existing glazed perimeter wall, form an overall U-shape of raw office space. Within this area, the primary form is a thick wall of office partitions that three-dimensionally curves, bends, and folds its way in an arc from one end of the space to another. Classic Morphosis design combines a singular striking gesture with fluid forms, a strong materials palette, and a sense of discovery as visitors walk through the space.

The space enclosed by the concave arc of the tube and the orthogonal core block contains the flexible conference/work areas, singular architectural events of implied enclosure and material specificity. Between the outside edges of the tube and the existing exterior wall are the offices requiring complete privacy. The computer/conference area at the southwest corner is an isolated event. The bank of private offices is disrupted for the rotated platonic volume containing the computers and an interstitial conference/work area to occur at the glazed wall. Solid form freestanding team rooms include fragments of gypsum board and nylon scrims providing some translucency. These are draped over cantilevered steel pipes and supported by steel cables. The scrim material, also appearing adjacent to the entry bridge and as an enclosure for the computer room, makes a backing for graphics. As a visual pun, a computer graphic of Morphosis' rendering of the space is printed on one of the team room's scrims. The client's graphics are displayed throughout the space in contrast to the neutral palette of metal and white. Except for the Aeron chairs, all of the furniture was designed by Morphosis and the steel fabricator was Tom Farrange & Co.

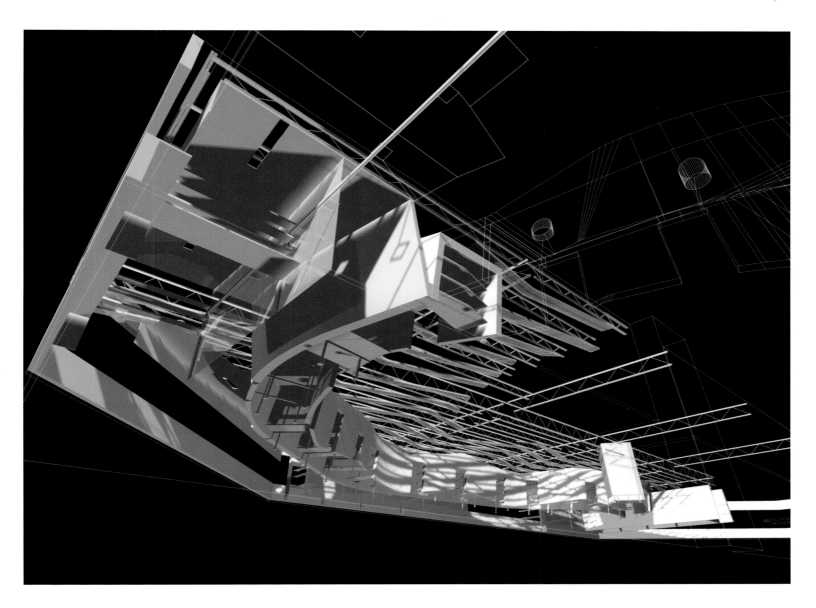

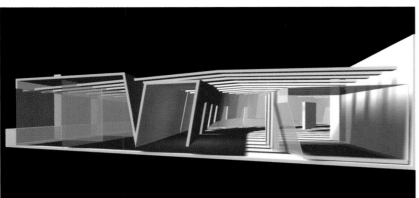

In sharp contrast to the bland spec building in which it is housed, SHR's offices are characterized by a strong interior design statement.

The sculptural spine accommodates offices ranging from 70 to 200 square feet (6.5 to 19 square meters) for the creative staff. Doorless areas have built-in custom furniture and recessed incandescent lighting.

The main conference area, an architectural and engineering feat, occupies a space with a thirty-five-foot-high (10.7-meter) central shaft that pierces the floor above and is capped with a skylight. A sixteen-foot-long (4.9-meter) glass and steel table is suspended with cables from a steel beam. Also suspended are cast-fiberglass pods impregnated with aluminum filings that help provide acoustic precision; or else the room would be a giant echo chamber.

Secondary themes—both material and spatial in nature—simultaneously confront, oppose, and reinforce the primary gesture of demarcation. Each of the three conference-work areas inside the white "tube" of workstations is an oasis of distinct material presence. The office entrance from the generic elevator lobby is a dynamic and complex procession with a double-height volume from below and a material/spatial axis sliced through the "tube" toward the computer volume and the outdoors beyond. The ceiling-scape is woven together with linear folded screens of perforated metal that float above the interstitial work area. Suspended from the twelve-foot-high (3.7-meter) plane, they seem to have their own rhythm and logic. Attached to the bottoms of the existing trusses, they reveal the architecture of the generic shell within which a particular genius locus is established.

As form and function work together in this space, neither is neglected. As Barry Shepard, a principal and co-founder of the twenty-nine-year-old firm SHR Perceptual Management, can attest to: "All of our concerns evaporated and we were pleasantly surprised."

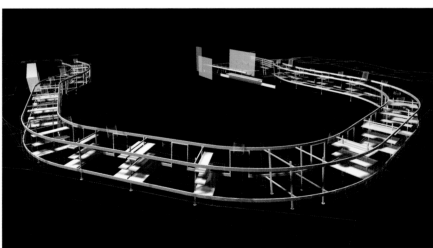

The sculptural spine accommodates offices ranging from 70 to 200 square feet (6.5 to 19 square meters) for the creative staff. Doorless areas have built-in custom furniture and recessed incandescent lighting.

The serpentine wall forms a bench opposite reception and provides a display area for product.

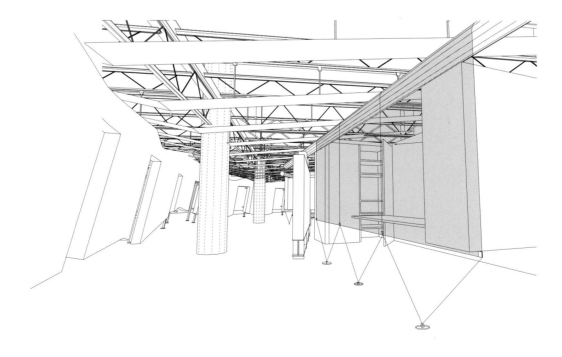

Located in Columbus, Ohio, the 1925 Smith Brothers Hardware building project is a remarkable instance of adaptive reuse of industrial architecture. The 210,000-square-foot (19,509-square-meter) landmark warehouse,

The 1925 Smith Brothers Hardware building, an adaptive reuse project, was presumed unsalvageable. RPA made every effort to preserve the historical integrity of the building while adapting it to their high-tech needs.

recalling the city's heyday of manufacturing and distribution, defied successful renovation for fourteen years and was presumed unsalvageable. The fire-ravaged and graffiti-strewn eyesore blotted the city's new airport-to-downtown artery until Retail Planning Associates (RPA) undertook the project to turn the building into its world headquarters.

Every effort was made to preserve the historical integrity of the building while adapting it to RPA's high-tech requirements. For instance, a piece of the merchandise chute used to send products, which were retrieved by roller-skating employees, from the top floors to the delivery desks on the first, is an objet trouvee in the building's lobby. The cavity left by the chute was used to house electrical lines and computer cables so the building could be updated with minimal disruption to its historical character. Another example, the two hundred ten windows could not be preserved without energy inefficiency, and replacement windows that had double panes were located. Though more expensive than storefront or undivided windows, they preserved the original appearance of the building. Floor plans were devised that permitted 72 percent of the windows—and natural light—to be part of common space.

The bricks covering the concrete edifice were in need of significant repair. The beautifully variegated brick was fired as a paver brick, larger than those commonly used for walls, and was no longer available. Their distinctive color and size made finding a commercially available replacement impossible. Through a nationwide search, RPA's materials experts located 16,000 bricks in Nelsonville, Ohio, where they were manufactured, in the backyard of someone's home. The entire building was draped in scaffolding and Visqueen to allow masons to restore all brick that had been damaged or incorrectly patched.

The water tower, once used to catch rainwater to power the building's gravity-fed sprinkler system, offered RPA a chance to brand the building while also preserving its history. During the renovation, the company had developed a new corporate identity and the water tower would be one of the first uses of the new mark. Lighting engineers employed the software Lightscape to backlight the brand name, throw light through the water tower legs, and crown the top with a purple corona that airplane passengers descending into Columbus regard as a beacon. The historic name banners have been reinscribed across the four brick faces.

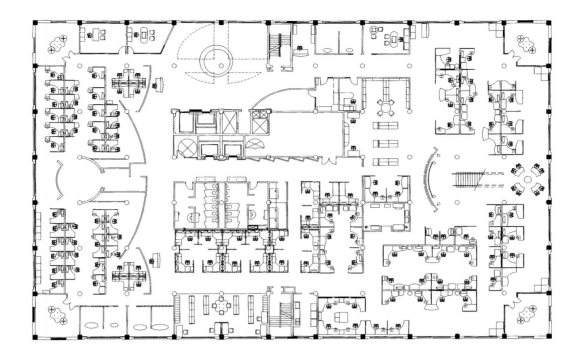

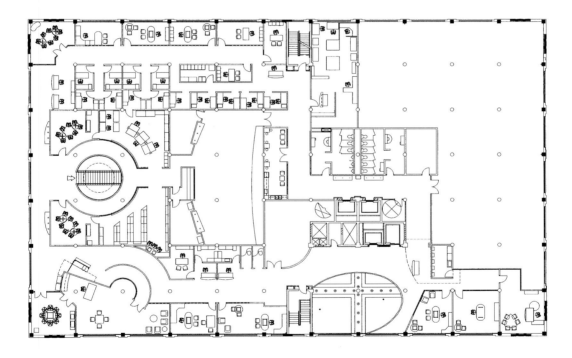

Floor plans were devised that permit 72 percent of the windows—and natural light—to be part of common space.

The concrete columns supporting the building, spaced every twenty feet (6.1 meters) and tapering from approximately three feet (0.9 meters)in diameter in the basement to eighteen inches (46 centimeters) on the sixth floor, were left exposed (some even with graffiti) and used as focal points or spatial rhythmic elements.

The building's annex, a loading dock built in 1927, was salvaged as well to soften the contours of the 210,000-square-foot (19,509-square-meter) box. With so much of the area preserved, Columbus Downtown Development Office dedicated $425,000 in capital improvements to public property around the site.

For the interior, the design studio's ever-changing project team alignments were accommodated by the installation of a Knoll office system, whose rice paper-like panels include wire management, power distribution housing, and modularity. Concrete floor cuts visually unite the fifth and sixth floors and symbolize the synergies of a consultancy that takes its design notions all the way from social science-based strategic rationale to drafting board to client presentation board to bricks and mortar.

More essentially, the perspective of the RPA client is adopted by RPA designers so the inner workings of a retail design consultancy,and RPA's latest foray into retail high-tech might be rendered comprehensible, even captivating. RPA's New Media division, as a consequence, installed a Touchscreen wall in an enclave designed especially for pausing with clients to explain computer-age consumerism. A zigzag wall of tonal greens and cantilevered halogen lamps transform the inert space of a corridor into an opportunity for arraying the developmental stages of a project, so the transliteration of research findings into design details can be witnessed firsthand by visiting CEOs. The visual resource room containing two million slides of the best and worst class of retail design around the globe is housed behind glass partitions so their review and preparation at light tables for clients can be observed.

Whimsy and reverie are intermittently permitted in swirling, sloping walls that wrap into an office conch shell, and violet light washes that spray the soffit-encircled space of the ceiling. The dolphins above the fountain were fashioned by a senior RPA designer from corrugated metal roofing and trashcan lids.

The adaptive reuse of old materials proved cost-effective. Most class A office buildings average $100 to $110 per square foot in Columbus. Smith Brothers Hardware costs approximately $70. Practically speaking, a fast-track renovation plan was devised for the project, fitting what would have been a two-year project into eleven-and-a-half weeks. All renovation happened alongside regular business, testing fully—and proving—RPA's strategy, design, and implementation capabilities.

RPA's latest venture into retail high-tech includes a New Media division. A permanently installed touchscreen wall in an enclave was designed especially for pausing with clients to explain computer-age consumerism.

The visual resource room contains two million slides and is housed behind glass partitions so their review and preparation for clients at light tables can be observed.

The decorative dolphins were made by a senior RPA designer from corrugated metal roofing and trashcan lids.

When **Sofinnova,** a venture capitalist firm with strong ties to Europe that **specializes in high-tech and bio-tech up-starts,** decided to relocate their offices **to Union Square,**

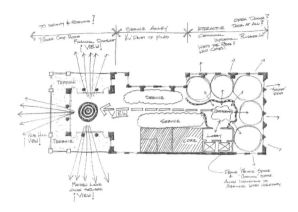

San Francisco's bustling retail district adjacent to the financial core, they went from a modern high rise to an industrial downtown space. The company had always been housed in temporary offices and was unfamiliar with the renovation and design process. They asked the new building's landlord who was currently renovating the rest of the building. The answer: Huntsman Architectural Group. After a series of meetings and interviews, they hired the firm to work on their project. "We just clicked," says Huntsman Architectural Group's design partner Mark Harbick. "The client seemed so nice and fun."

Indeed, the project turned out to be enjoyable for both architect and client. The 4,300-square-foot (126-square-meter) penthouse atop an early-twentieth-century landmark building came complete with twenty-foot (6.1-meter) ceiling heights, an influx of natural light, incredible views of the city, and a terrace protected from the wind. Recently, the building had been renovated and seismically reinforced; the presence of brick, concrete, and steel appealed to Sofinnova. Missing links provided included cabling and power for electronic communications, mechanical equipment, and sprinklers.

Huntsman Architectural Group, including Harbick as well as project designers John Seamon and Laura Plasberg, was given the challenge of creating a look that would be appropriate for a forward-thinking venture capitalist investing in high-technology. The goal was to look innovative without pretense. The client wanted to retain the open, loft-like feel of the central space, but with private offices for the partners. "However," says Harbick, "we went back and forth a few times about how people in the company actually function. We found out that they don't need a lot of privacy and traditional office space. They

mostly leave doors open and talk among themselves." Only on occasion does the office host important presentations. So, the client and architect determined that while there was no need for a receptionist station, the space required a comfortable lounge with a computer hook-up. Meetings for ten or more people as well as smaller groups needed to be accommodated, so a conference room was designed and includes a Poulsen pendant light above the table that has been described as "an architectural folly at the end of an axis."

To preserve daylight and create several private offices, Harbick selected polygal (extruded polycarbonate) for the office walls. The material could be manipulated for the tall spaces and costs less than traditional solid gypsum walls and significantly less than glass walls. Light from exterior windows suffuses the interior spaces. With the large pivot doors open, the original brick walls and steel seismic beams are revealed as well as views of San Francisco's skyline. The most dramatic display of brightness, says Harbick, is when visitors cross the dark elevator lobby area and step into the light-filled reception area. "Like a crystalline box," he says.

Harbick left remnants of terra cotta on the ceiling, rough concrete (now epoxy-coated) flooring, exposed brick walls, and steel beams, rid of paint and primer exposing original black cast. "We had a lot of people working on ridding the place of primer," says Harbick. "And that's not easy. Primer is made to withstand anything." Aside from the acrylic partitions, oversized 12 ft. x 4 ft. (3.7 m x 1.2 m) doors, cabinetry, and a linear cherry credenza run down the central promenade and connect with the terrace-ringed conference room. Small sconces above every file unit continue, when the wall stops, as down-spots emanating from a suspended "light beam" of stainless steel. "The partners are all very interested in art and have collected wonderful work," says Harbick. "The walls around the copy and lunch rooms are tall and blank. They are reserved for large canvases, while the space below the cherry bookcases are for a smaller, black-and-white photography collection." Another collectible sits in one of the partners' office—a herbivore fish, allegedly living 85 million years ago.

As the project came to an end, Harbick and his team asked the client about future needs. "They were pretty sure about not growing or expanding," recalls Harbick. "But I knew better." Lo and behold, the company has hired three more partners and is debating whether to completely abandon the space and move or build out. Either way, it looks like Huntsman Architectural Group has work ahead.

Looking across the file alignment in the corridor to the partner's office with seismic brace. The light fixtures are hung steel troughs.

The reception/lounge area is complete with 12 ft. x 4 ft. (3.7 m x 1.2 m) custom doors and translucent partitions.

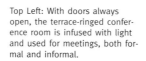

Top Left: With doors always open, the terrace-ringed conference room is infused with light and used for meetings, both formal and informal.

Bottom Left: Huntsman Architectural Group did not want to spoil the offices' incredible views and left the windows untreated.

Top Right: Seismic braces were left as a design detail in partners' offices.

Bottom Right: Walls were left bare to accommodate the partners' art collection. Custom cabinetry and filing systems were done by a company called DFM.

One partner at Sofinnova had to accommodate his pet herbivore fish, said to be 85 million years old, into the design scheme.

Top and Bottom Right: The warmth of the cherry custom filing system is enhanced when the daylight seeps through the acrylic partitions.

Unlike the violent 1971 film Straw Dogs with Dustin Hoffman and Susan George, **two quietly straightforward words** describe Jesse Dylan's Los Angeles commercial production company of the same name: **progressive and understated.**

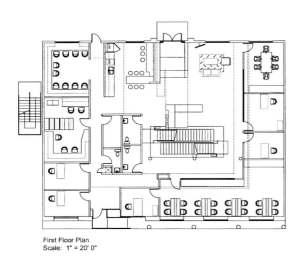

First Floor Plan
Scale: 1" = 20' 0"

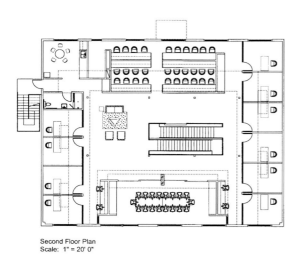

Second Floor Plan
Scale: 1" = 20' 0"

⊗ William Emmerson teamed with Pugh + Scarpa to create 10,000 square feet of space for the production company.

Moving east from cramped Santa Monica quarters, Dylan fell for a freestanding structure on Third Street near Sweetzer. His plan: demolish the old interior and create an open space that could easily accommodate the company without significant architectural changes. He continues to state that he did not want the space to seem overdesigned—form had to follow function. Like all good plans, this one changed. The original project team, William Emmerson and co-contractors Hinerfeld-Ward and Binder/Minardos Builders, found that the 10,000-square-foot (929-square-meter) space inspired them to broaden their vision. Suddenly, the project turned into a full-scale renovation process with serious architectural plans. The Los Angeles firm Pugh & Scarpa were called upon to bring the ideas into reality.

Working with a basic brick industrial shell, the team punctured the roof with a skylight and added a gentle ramp and canopy-like soffit that now stretches from the parking lot to the office center, where the reception desk, made of interlocking strips of Douglas Fir solids, and focal double staircase stand. The client was adamant about the double staircase, as it figured prominently into his original vision. However, Dylan's beloved stairway underwent quite a few reincarnations before the project team settled on the final design. Combining high-tech and high-touch, the stairway features a cantilever of continuous sheets of folded metal, tubular steel supports, stainless-steel cables, and a mahogany handrail.

The architects, led by principal Gwynne Pugh, developed a scheme that inverted certain traditional precepts. The executive and conference areas are on the upper level. The ground floor houses support services and high-tech editing bays. Reinforcing the company's egalitarian views, executive offices are organized against the building's windowless walls while editing, production, administrative, and conference areas line the windowed elevations. On both floors, central spaces play an important roll. Lounge settings and an open kitchen support a communal environment, and the floor plans are virtually corridor-free. Much of the second floor is planned as an open space and has the atmosphere of a living room. Indirect lighting, ductwork, and wiring are accommodated in a soffit that is incorporated into the framing system.

The dramatic double staircase is made with cantilevered sheets of folded metal, tubular steel supports, stainless-steel cables, and handrails of Honduras mahogany.

The custom-designed reception desk, made by Emmerson himself, is fabricated from interlocking strips of Douglas fir.

Drawing on references from Rudolph Schindler and traditional Japanese design, the team built office partitions with Douglas fir frames incorporating doors. In addition, combinations of medium-density fiberboard and gridded glass address the workplace issue of privacy versus openness. Similarly, gridded pocket doors, partially fitted with panels of sandwiched glass from local company Fred's Glass, front the twenty-two-foot-long (6.7-meter) conference room, which can be divided by full-height by sliding Honduras mahogany panels.

The team also respected the building's industrial history, concrete flooring, a wood-beamed ceiling, and the new structural components create a recessive background for the dominant stairway and the furnishings. These elements create character and define a certain spirit as well as distinguish it from countless other facilities around town. The building itself inspired the space's furnishing choices. With an eye for quality and quirky, William Emmerson, who owns the Melrose Avenue shop Emmerson Troop, assembled a grouping of vintage pieces that span several decades. In addition, he included original work of his own. The result could have been a miscellaneous assemblage. However, the outcome is original and colorful with a sense of fun. For example, steel-framed chairs from the 1950s are reupholstered in acid-green fabric and lit by Achille Castiglioni and Pier Giacomo's Arco lamp. The reception seating sits on Francesca Turner's 1947 rug, which, until recently, was a wall hanging in a Neutra house. A poured-in-place concrete bench on the lower level and Emmerson's screen made of pivoting mahogany panels updates the vibe. On the second floor, vintage Knoll, a Noguchi table, Kem Weber seating (in original vinyl), Paul Frankl chairs, and a bunch of George Nelson bubble lamps keep it simple and timeless, says Emmerson.

In keeping with the rest of the understated design scheme, the waiting/lounge area is fitted out in comfortable, modern furnishings.

With a Japanese-like design, the conference room includes sliding mahogany panels. The vintage chairs sit around a zebra wood tabletop and a vintage Herman Miller base.

The open-space, second floor has a relaxed, living room scheme with indirect lighting, duct work, and wiring built into a soffit that is incorporated into the framing system.

When architecture firm **Gould Evans** Associates

in Phoenix began to grow beyond its walls in its former home, firm leaders **started a search for new digs.**

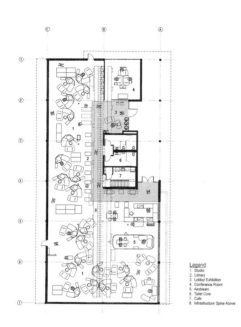

Floor plan and elevation for
GEA's new Phoenix office.

Legend
1. Studio
2. Library
3. Lobby/ Exhibition
4. Conference Room
5. Airstream
6. Toilet Core
7. Cafe
8. Infrastructure Spine Above

They knew that whether they would lease or buy, they needed something with "good bones" that could be the stage for the experimental workplace that they had in mind. The studio had to encourage out-of-the-box thinking and provocative design solutions; they wanted to support an open dialogue among staff; and create a space to test materials and model making. "We wanted it to be like a manufacturing plant," says Phoenix principal Jay Silverberg. "We wanted staff and clients to be able to see building materials, mock ups, and computer plans in the studio at all times." And when your clients include a local college with plans for a state-of-the-art computer lab and media classroom, bringing tech design into an educational format requires interactive meetings.

Shopping around in Phoenix, the design team came upon a nondescript 1960s building on Third Avenue. The 7,000-square-foot building had been multi-tenanted for years, and was divided into many offices. But principals Trudi Hummel, Jay Silverberg, and Bob Gould saw potential. "Even then we could see that the building had a wonderful spirit representative of its time," says Silverberg. "We felt that we could strip it down and reveal the quality of its original structure." Uncovering the essence of the structure appealed to the group; it seemed as though it could provide an excellent backdrop for the new workspace.

Adapting an existing building appealed to the group as an efficient, conscientious choice, and committing to the midtown neighborhood was important. "We looked at all kinds of properties," says Gould, "and decided that purchasing a building here was an opportunity to contribute to a neighborhood revitalization. Being an investor in the physical fabric of the city is part of Gould Evans' mission."

After the dramatic renovation that exposed the concrete tee roof structure, the transformed building began to represent other aspects of the firm's mission. The open studio environment supports creativity and a teamwork-based approach to design and client service. There are virtually no walls in the space and teams can be reconfigured quickly because everything is on wheels.

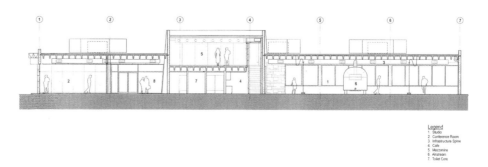

Legend
1. Studio
2. Conference Room
3. Infrastructure Spine
4. Cafe
5. Mezzanine
6. Airstream
7. Toilet Core

The challenge: How to handle the data and mechanical/electrical infrastructure while emphasizing mobility. The Gould Evans design team, which also included Steve Fucello, Donna Barry, Tom Reilly, Karen Gould, Jose Pombo, Tamara Shroll, and Neil Sommers, created voice/data hubs that can be moved to accommodate groups of workstations. "The infrastructure armature is the organizing mechanism," Silverberg explains. "It's kind of similar to an umbilical cord." All of the voice, data, and computer electronics are displayed and exposed, visible in a raw state, but always moving. "There is no sense of permanence in the space," says Silverberg. "Technology goes where we need it. Plus, we can bring a client right into an area where their project is being worked on and bring them into the design process."

The synergistic culture in the office breeds a high level of design and client service. "The open, vibrant environment is representative of our horizontal organization," says Hummel. "We stay plugged into what each team is doing, and aware of the nuances of each project. This reinforces our philosophy of collaboration."

The office is also a demonstration space. "We're pushing the limits of how you can achieve flexibility," Hummel says, "which is something every client is looking for in some way." The office is also a place to test new or unusual materials, such as resource-efficient hand-sanded Homosote board and translucent Polygal panels, and many other inexpensive, high-durability materials.

The team knew they'd need a place for the sometimes-necessary private conversation or meeting, and a vintage Airstream turned out to be the unlikely solution. Purchased from someone's backyard in North Kansas City, the 1945 classic was gutted, outfitted, polished, re-wired, and driven to Phoenix. A few details were left untouched: the curtain rods now hang drawings with clips and at night, the tail lights emit a glow that light up the front window.

Does the office work? A month ago, a multiple team reconfiguration meant that all 27 people in the office would have to move. In a traditional space this could take weeks and cost a great deal in materials and time. On Third Avenue, it took just four hours.

The open studio environment at Gould Evans Associates' Phoenix office supports creativity, state-of-the-art technology, and a teamwork-based work approach.

GEA's Phoenix office is a place to test materials, such as translucent Polygal panels like the ones used in the reception/gallery/lobby space, and steel, as shown in the staircase made of a piece of naturally finished steel plate.

GEA's Phoenix office is a place to test materials, such as translucent Polygal panels like the ones used in the reception/gallery/lobby space, and steel, as shown in the staircase made of a piece of naturally finished steel plate.

The firm needed a place for private meetings—a vintage Airstream turned out to be the unlikely solution; purchased, polished, and wired, it's an entire office on wheels.

Ben Franklin proved that electricity could be channeled from the sky using a simple, small wooden model with a removable roof and collapsible walls hinged at the base.

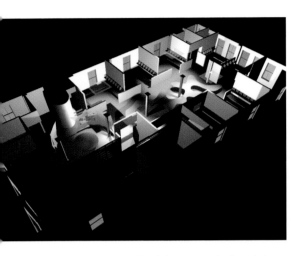

A lightning rod ran up the gable and ended in a detachable brass ball above the chimney. Inside, he placed a cup of gunpowder. When in contact with the electrical current, an explosion occurred. Franklin called this a House of Thunder.

The online marketing and communications company, Thunder House, owned and operated by McCann-Erickson Worldwide, specializes in website strategy and design and describes itself as "a convergence of different attitudes and sensibilities. These varied sensibilities create a dynamic atmosphere where whatever moves through is a result of not one individual but the influence of many."

Understanding both Ben Franklin's scientific theory and the namesake company's work ethic, Resolution: 4 Architecture took on the project—Thunder House's new 5,000-square-foot (465-square-meter) office space. Located in New York City's Chelsea neighborhood, the headquarters occupies the top floor (twelfth) of an old loft warehouse. According to Thunder House's director Amanda Richmond, the company currently employs nine people but is expected to grow to thirty-five within two years. The Internet company required a design solution capable of sustaining such rapid growth in an overall process of ten weeks and a budget of $135,000. Joseph Tanney and Robert Luntz, partners in Resolution: 4 Architecture, and the architects for the parent company's premises, were called upon to work some quick magic. With the help of project architects Setu Shah and Mike Sweebe and a one-man project team consisting of Brian Bowman, the group maintained their practice's long-held commitment to the incorporation of the latest technology—Mac-based CAD programs for both the design and documentation—to expedite the design process.

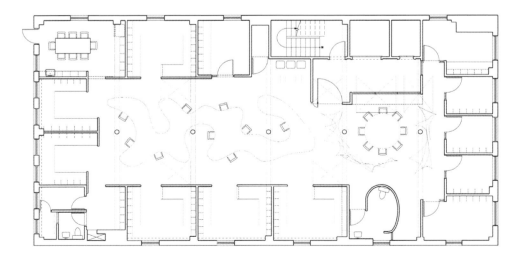

⊘ Low-acrylic partitions measuring four-, five-, or seven-feet (1.2, 1.5, or 2.1-meter) high, create an envelope wrapping the perimeter that define semiprivate offices for the creative team.

The space was gutted except a curved bathroom enclosure, which soon became the inspiration for the interior scheme. Skylit, an entry portal (or walk-in point) made of corrugated metal and acrylic translucent panels that project a warm glow provides a transition for visitors between the time they step off the elevator and move through the oversized, pivoting front door that measures 7 ft. x 6 ft. (2.1 m x 1.8 m). Once inside, private offices for accountants and money managers occupy the north end of the space, while a series of low-acrylic partitions measuring four-, five-, or seven-feet high, create an envelope wrapping the perimeter that define semiprivate offices for the creative team, each measuring approximately 165 square feet (15 square meters). The open, communal space has overhead linear blue lights that reference computer screens and the idea of the digital. Fabricated on site from full-scale drawings, a forty-foot (12.2-meter) custom Baltic birch table weaves its way around columns, knitting together the work area that accommodates website production. Designed to literally link ten people, the table seats Web designers and a receptionist.

Installed by designer and noted tent maker Gisela Stromeyer, a conference area, where final client presentations are made, is defined by an annular overlapping of Lycra panels stretched to create an ephemeral volume with visual privacy and make-shift projection screens. The overlapping fabric leaves narrow slits between the folds for entry access and a warm glow of incandescent lighting washes over the space.

Like most new media ventures, the client worried about an inevitable workforce explosion. So, both the birch table and the creative offices allow for added seating—moving easily from a single to shared occupancy.

"Ben built his Thunder House to prove that electricity could be channeled from the sky," say both Tanney and Luntz. "This Thunder House is an interactive agency responsible for creating electrifying websites, interactive media campaigns, and marketing programs for high-energy clients." The architects conclude that design decisions were made not only in adherence to the tight budget and schedule, but also to articulate the convergence of such ideas.

A forty-foot (12.2-meter), custom Baltic birch table weaves its way around columns, knitting together the work area that accommodates Web site production. It links ten people, Web designers, and a receptionist.

Installed by Gisela Stromeyer, a conference area is defined by an annular overlapping of Lycra panels stretched to create an ephemeral volume with visual privacy and make-shift projection screens.

Upshot, a progressive and rapidly growing marketing agency, recently collaborated with SPACE to create their Chicago headquarters. "Originally, Upshot was located in a brownstone

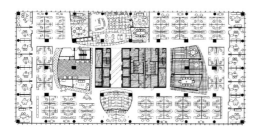

Top and Bottom: SPACE created 50,000 square feet (4,645 square meters) of new offices for Upshot, and is adding another 60,000 square feet (5,574 square meters) to accommodate growth.

that they had renovated themselves," says Dana Hegedorn, the project's senior designer. "After a major fire and under great duress, they came to us for help. They had just landed a big account, SONY, and needed to expand, and they had taken up residence in a bar across the street."

Hegedorn and her team put the company up in temporary digs and took a Post-it approach to design for this location. However, when it came to the permanent space, a straightforward design process that included 50,000 square feet (4,645 square meters) was in the works. (Subsequently, Upshot, with the help of SPACE, is adding another 60,000 square feet (5,574 square meters) on a new floor.) Managed like a marketing assignment, complete with a project mission statement and a teaser campaign to excite employees, the result successfully communicates the kinetic and energetic agency culture.

The conventional, corporate glass box base building is juxtaposed when the elevator doors open to the first of two Upshot floors and enter the reception area. Employees and visitors are flooded with color, movement, video, and music that plays twenty-four hours a day; all of the senses are bombarded. A board lights up the reception area with various rotating messages. Also in the lobby, a signage billboard that depicts something speeding through a tunnel, so as to feel like you are catapulted into the space. The ceiling, left open, exposes wiring, ducts, and pipes, accentuating ceiling height and eluding to a loft environment. As Hegedorn says, the scheme maintains the honesty of the structure.

Throughout the space, the finishes are a little bit harder, more grown up in the lobby area but then get progressively creative as you go through the space. Using very few right angles, the design team utilized curved walls that are painted with various patterns and colors. This keeps a sense of orientation. "You always know where you are by looking around because no two walls are the same," says Hegedorn.

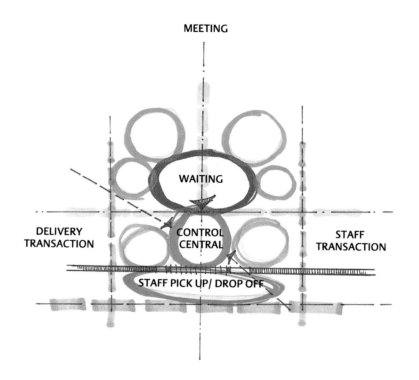

MEETING

WAITING

DELIVERY
TRANSACTION

CONTROL
CENTRAL

STAFF
TRANSACTION

STAFF PICK UP/ DROP OFF

RECEPTION ZONING

The scheme is based on an energy concept and this kinetic concept reinvented how Upshot employees work. Brainstorming rooms, named by function, offer distinct meeting and technology scenarios appropriate to all types of interactions. An informal charrette might happen in Spark; a team meeting is held in Ignition or Plug; and a client presentation is held in Reactor, the state-of-the-art presentation room. Fuel doubles as the lunch lounge and after-hours bar with the beer tap. Off allows someone to get away from the fast pace and collect a thought.

While energetic and collaborative spaces serve the process well, personal focus spaces allow a copywriter time to develop a story, a creative director space to illustrate the story, and an account manager privacy to phone the client. Knoll Currents stations with taller panels on three sides and one open teaming side provide focus space and yet keep the team connected. The Knoll Currents aesthetic and unusual technology capacity is a perfect match to brand Upshot. Though many employees work at open stations and are encouraged to express themselves by displaying stuffed animals or action figures, private offices are reserved for vice presidents and senior vice presidents.

For a company that experienced such a rapid growth period with a young staff, the idea is to create the unconventional; no product that comes out of any department is something that has been done before. By studying the work process and understanding the Upshot culture, SPACE created a user-friendly home for the Upshot employee and a dynamic innovative space for the visitor.

RECEPTION

1000
sf

The conventional, corporate glass box base building is juxtaposed when the elevator doors open to the first of two Upshot floors and enter the reception area.

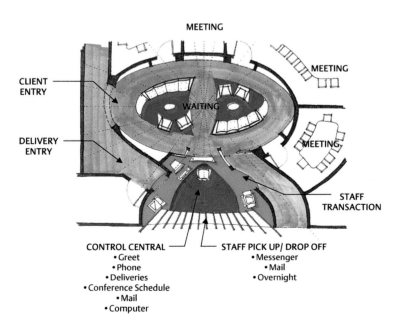

MEETING

MEETING

CLIENT
ENTRY

WAITING

DELIVERY
ENTRY

MEETING

STAFF
TRANSACTION

CONTROL CENTRAL
• Greet
• Phone
• Deliveries
• Conference Schedule
• Mail
• Computer

STAFF PICK UP/ DROP OFF
• Messenger
• Mail
• Overnight

THE HANG OUT

1800 SF

⊗ Fuel doubles as the lunch lounge and after hours bar with the beer tap.

⊘ The Hang Out provides R + R for employees.

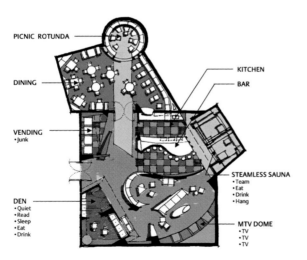

PICNIC ROTUNDA

DINING

KITCHEN

BAR

VENDING
• Junk

STEAMLESS SAUNA
• Team
• Eat
• Drink
• Hang

DEN
• Quiet
• Read
• Sleep
• Eat
• Drink

MTV DOME
• TV
• TV
• TV

PRIVATE OFFICE

OPEN WORKSPACE

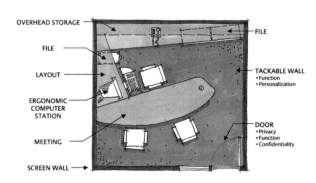

OVERHEAD STORAGE

FILE

FILE

LAYOUT

TACKABLE WALL
• Function
• Personalization

ERGONOMIC
COMPUTER
STATION

MEETING

DOOR
• Privacy
• Function
• Confidentiality

SCREEN WALL

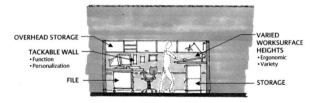

OVERHEAD STORAGE

TACKABLE WALL
• Function
• Personalization

FILE

VARIED
WORKSURFACE
HEIGHTS
• Ergonomic
• Variety

STORAGE

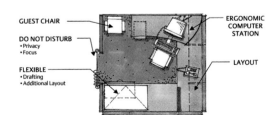

GUEST CHAIR

DO NOT DISTURB
• Privacy
• Focus

FLEXIBLE
• Drafting
• Additional Layout

ERGONOMIC
COMPUTER
STATION

LAYOUT

Knoll Currents stations with taller
panels on three sides and one
open teaming side provide focus
space and yet keep the team
connected.

In the emerging high-tech world, architects and designers need to respond to **specific needs** and increasingly find they have to combine these wishes with **global necessities.** Take for example **William T. Georgis'** latest endeavor.

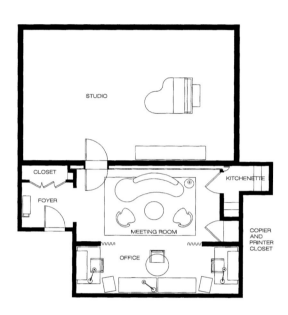

The New York-based architect, who worked with Robert Venturi and Robert A.M. Stern before establishing his own firm in 1992, recently developed an office for an international business dedicated to developing videoconferencing communication systems for educators, musicians, and arts administrators to exceed physical gaps and reach with global audiences. Videoconferencing, a technology that allows people to see, hear, speak, and share documents and information with associates in various worldwide locations and in real time, took on the central role as a design element. However, Georgis also had to weave into the scheme a welcoming feel so that visitors would feel relaxed among the digital and the arts.

For this project, the issues include creating an elegant and functional space that can accommodate an excess of high-tech gadgets, such as cameras, VCRs, large-screen television monitors, and scan converters. Also, Georgis was asked to create a comfortable, flexible workspace for office and meeting functions. The client had already built a music conferencing studio on site and Georgis had to accommodate the existing facility.

One of the major elements of the project was light. Georgis had inherited a windowless space and wanted to create a warm environment without natural daylight. The architect's answer was to create a metaphorical window, a backlit glass wall along the divide between the meeting and studio rooms. Once the area was lit, Georgis played around with materials that would impart a sense of theater. "Overall, we aimed to create sleek and tailored modern interiors as to complement the wide range of classical music that is performed and discussed here," says Georgis.

The office is clad in ebonized oak. Floors are concrete with baseboards of brushed stainless steel. Set up to accommodate three staff members, the office is in two symmetrical areas with a circular table at midpoint. The polished aluminum bases and glass tops of the Burdick desk system brighten up the dark space. Silk curtains with a red crushed-velvet lining divide the office space from the meeting room, which can become an informal meeting area after conferences. The meeting area was created as a more "lounge" space than official conference center. Included in the space are modern classics from Jacobsen and Eames as well as a Vladimir Kagan sofa and a 1950s orange Murano light fixture. Ebonized wood and glass walls complete the look.

The client wanted a sleek and tailored modern space for musicians and enthusiasts to meet.

A pantry and closets (for copy machines and printers) are concealed in spatial recess. The videoconferencing room and music studio, with its own grand piano, also serve as a space for the chairman and founder of the business to conduct master classes when he is in New York. The space also functions as an informal salon for classical musicians.

Georgis' project is an office that exemplifies the capabilities of advanced technologies in the service of education and the arts. Combining high-tech with fine art and traditional office needs, Georgis was able to develop a holistic approach to design.

This page and facing page: Silk curtains with a red crushed-velvet lining divide the office space from the meeting room, which became an informal meeting area. The meeting area was created as a more "lounge" space than official conference center.

Peter Sisson, founder of **Wineshopper.com,** an e-commerce company that offers **wines to consumers through its website,** retained San Francisco-based Huntsman Architectural Group to

design the company's locations in Napa Valley and San Francisco after a local broker recommended the firm. "Peter called and we met pretty quickly," says John Seamon, the project architect/designer. "He has a brain larger than a boulder and a vocabulary that includes phrases like 'Dynamite' and 'Right on.' He is a computer science graduate from Dartmouth and [has] an MBA from Stanford. I knew immediately that we could work together."

The project follows the trend towards blending the look of a company's office with its brand and product. The San Francisco site serves as the headquarters for Wineshopper.com's in-house engineering, sales, and marketing functions, while the Napa facility includes customer service and development. A third facility, also in Napa Valley and designed by Huntsman Architectural Group, houses central shipping, receiving, and order fulfillment.

Initially, the Huntsman Architectural Group was hired to work on the San Francisco site, 7,500 square feet (697 square meters), and the Napa site, 13,000 square feet (1,208 square meters), through the schematic phase and into the design stage. Huntsman began to formulate ideas that seemed particular to the client's corporate culture. Sisson wanted to use eco-friendly materials whenever possible. As a result, Seamon incorporated those elements into the design. For example, the workstations, from Oakland-based Studio EG, are created almost entirely from recycled materials including wheatboard work surfaces and panels made from recycled newspaper.

Other design inspirations came from the great outdoors and reflect the rolling hills of wine country. An open-plan approach was used in the design of offices allowing for spacious work areas and numerous soft dividing elements. The reception areas in both locations include a unique hanging quilted wall separating reception from nearby open sections. The bright yellow color of this quilt represents the wild mustard blooms that cover the valley vineyards in spring. Other functional spaces, such as conference rooms and production areas, are clad in a translucent material to allow light to filter in.

⊘ The reception areas in both the
⊘ Napa and San Francisco locations
⊗ include a yellow hanging quilted
wall that separates the reception
from nearby open sections.

Spaces for private offices and small conference rooms were designed to standout from other spaces as an abstracted solid form, reminiscent of grape clusters.

Other functional spaces at the facilities, such as this conference room, are clad in a translucent material to allow light to filter in.

For the San Francisco office in particular, Seamon began with a typical shell found in the city's south of market district: the renovated warehouse was a concrete column and floor slab building with sixteen-foot ceilings (4.9-meter) and level changes where trains would dock. The confines of the space included 2 ft. x 2 ft. (0.6 m x 0.6 m) columns every fourteen feet (4.3 meters). "Our job was to go in to this very standard condition, leave the ceiling open, and from there transform it into the Wineshopper.com sensibility," says Seamon. This included three kinds of "forms" or environments/ enclosures/conditions. An abstracted solid form, reminiscent of grape clusters, became the spaces for private offices and small conference rooms. They were designed to stand out from other spaces. Concrete columns, spaced every twenty feet (6.1 meters), are used as focal points or spatial rhythmic elements. Whimsy and reverie are intermittently permitted in swirling, sloping walls that wrap into an office conch shell, and violet light washes that spray the soffit-encircled space of the ceiling.

The second type of space is a more pristine, clear, orthogonal enclosure. "More like the final product," says Seamon. "The distilled condition of something else; a refined final version of something." These spaces are used as meeting/collaboration areas. The third area, described by the designer as "in between constant mediation," are workstations set up like the rolling hills of nearby Napa with hanging dividers made of soft suede in a mustard yellow fabric. "It's like mediating rows of vines in the vineyards," says Seamon. The three areas provide an analogy to the wine making, representing the beginning (grapes), middle (mediation), and end (refinement) of the process.

The shell of the Napa facility was a new, tilt-up building, with fourteen- to twenty-four-foot (4.3-meter to 7.3-meter) ceilings, wide open spaces, and few obstructions. "It felt much more open, vacuous," says Seamon. The challenge here was to get the space filled vertically as well as create interesting elements from a sectional standpoint. The design team began to play with the idea of power and tele/data feeds to the workstations. Wanting to do more than just trench them into the floor or have power poles up to the ceiling, the team developed a vineyard spine that feeds all the work surfaces. It's success inspired the team to re-work the San Francisco space to include the same. Of course, what would the Napa office of Wineshopper.com be without a wine tasting lounge? Not much. So the team added one. Finally, in this facility, the meeting rooms are clad with walls and acrylic windows looking out over the vineyards.

The Wineshopper.com project is representative of clients looking for a new image through innovative and original design in this high-tech, high-turnover world, where the office environment plays a vital role in employee retention. Though the company has grown to two hundred thirty employees and six other sites, Sisson has put a curb on hiring, slowing down in the hopes of a possible future merger. Huntsman Architectural Group (Seamon in particular) is in the process of helping reorganize the company: "We are waiting for them to make the next move so we can be there to help them."

Huntsman Architectural Group created three work areas analogous to the wine making process: the beginning (grapes), middle (mediation), and end (refinement).

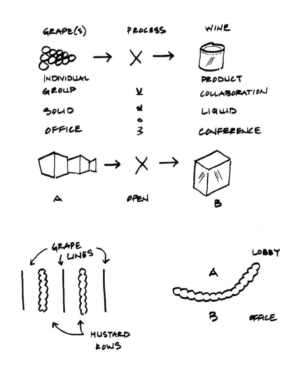

⊗ Top: The Napa office of Wineshopper.com had to include a wine tasting lounge that fit with the company's corporate culture and the space's design scheme.

⊗ Bottom Left: The shell of the Napa facility had fourteen- to twenty-four-foot ceilings (4.3-meter to 7.3-meter), wide-open spaces, and few obstructions. To solve the challenge of filling space vertically, as well as create interesting elements from a sectional standpoint, the designers created a mezzanine level.

⊗ Bottom Right: In the Napa facility, the meeting rooms are clad with walls and acrylic windows looking out over the vineyards.

Best-known for the **print magazine Wired,** Wired Ventures Inc. also has a new media component in its portfolio: **Wired Digital,** **the organization's cyber-side** that develops original Internet content and **provides a digital format for Wired's online venture.**

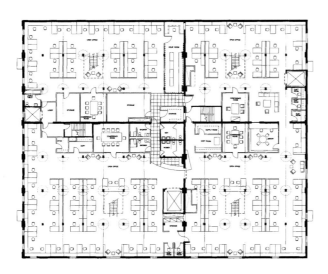

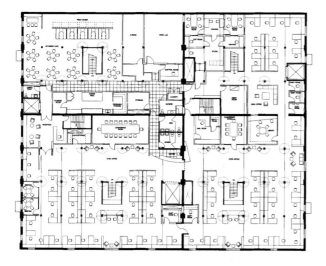

As expected, headquarters for such an endeavor are in an industrial warehouse in San Francisco's South of Market area, a magnet for new media matters. For John Holey, the design brains behind Wired's offices in San Francisco and New York, transforming the existing 1922 facility into one that would support a digital culture seemed like a simple plan.

Marked by an air of informality and a fresh-faced workforce (the average Wired employee age is twenty-four), the Wired Digital's corporate culture scorns traditional business and demands certain perks that must be woven into the interior design scheme. Also, in this particular new media case, Holey had to move two hundred thirty employees, who were previously housed on a 15,000-square-foot (1,394-square-meter) floor, to 44,000 square feet (4,088 square meters) spread over the top two floors of the site. Providing more breathing room may well have been the company's saving grace, but employees were afraid that the original site's dynamic spirit may have been lost in the larger space. Staff seemed to thrive on the close proximity and immediacy of the previous offices. Keeping that soul and upholding the client's mandates—provide adequate enclosures to counterbalance the open space but that there should not be private offices nor traditional panel systems—challenged Holey and his design team, which included Carl Bridges, Rob Wooding, Paul Dent, Joanne Beren, and Molly Johnson.

Existing masonry walls divided the floors into quadrants; the core would constitute the public circulation zone. Holey concentrated the enclosed areas, such as the conference rooms, library, production studio, media room, and storage area, along the main spine. Private circulation occurs within the workspaces, located at the window walls and at the skylit stairwells in each quadrant.

⊗ Two hundred and thirty employ-
⊗ ees, who were previously housed
on a 15,000-square-foot (1,394-
square-meter) floor, were moved
to 44,000 square feet (4,088
square meters) spread over
the top two floors of the new
industrial site.

The architect's first drawing of
Wired Digital.

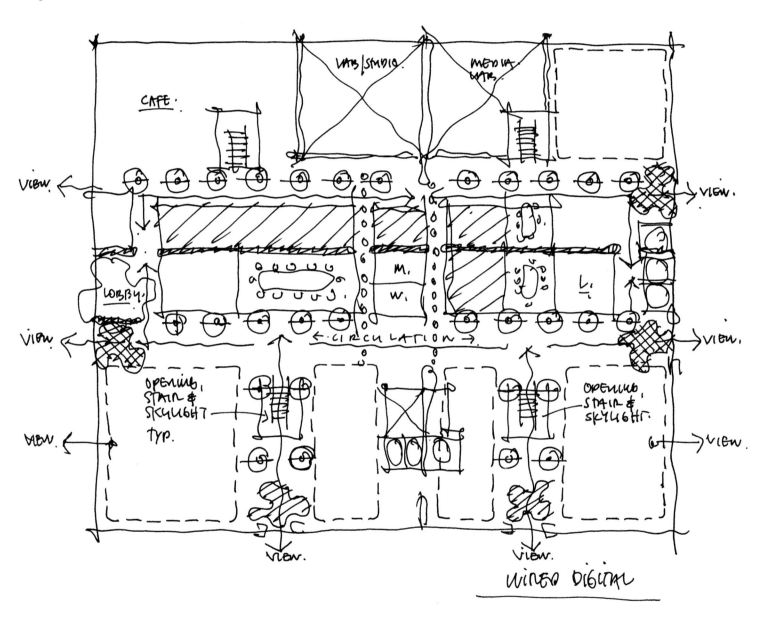

CAFE.

LAB/STUDIO.

MEDIA
LAB.

VIEW.

VIEW.

LOBBY.

VIEW.

VIEW.

← CIRCULATION →

OPENING,
STAIR &
SKYLIGHT
TYP.

OPENING,
STAIR &
SKYLIGHT.

VIEW.

VIEW.

VIEW.

VIEW.

WIRED DIGITAL

Having coined the phrase "office home," Holey created a low-tech atmosphere to contrast the high-tech nature of the company's work. The workstations are fashioned out of elementary materials— dividers are sheet metal studs securing forty-eight-inch-high (122- centimeter) sheets of clear-finished particleboard. Desks are made from file pedestals and solid core doors with particleboard legs. Also in each quadrant are lounge-like settings with soft seating for informal gatherings. Enclosed meeting rooms are also provided, as are glass-fronted conference rooms. In each area, relaxation spaces set the tone for employees: a café serves three meals a day, there is a bank of video games for fun; and a Z room with futons.

Though most of the budget went to infrastructure rehab, Holey stuck to $30 per square foot, including construction and workstations.

Skylights cap custom steel and wire mesh stairways that rises to face a glass-fronted meeting room.

Workstations are fashioned out of elementary materials—dividers are sheet metal studs securing forty-eight-inch-high (122-centimeter) sheets of clear-finished particleboard. Desks are made from file pedestals and solid core doors with particleboard legs.

Founded in 1998, Zefer, a leading strategic Internet consulting and services firm, works with both **established companies and dot.com start-ups** to create and execute

the glowing bar 2

FLOOR 4 - SCHEMATIC DESIGN A2

the grid

FLOOR 4 - SCHEMATIC DESIGN "C"

intersections

FLOOR 4 - SCHEMATIC DESIGN "D"

The four development plans of the Beach Street facility culminate in the final "Web" drawing.

strategies and adaptive new business models that thrive in the digital economy. "Our approach," says CEO William Seibel and company co-founder Anthony Tikan, "combines business strategy, experience, design, technology, and program management, allowing project teams to deliver tangible business results in a compressed time frame."

Headquartered in Boston with offices in Chicago, London, New York, Pittsburgh, and San Francisco, Zefer has more than six hundred fifty employees, all of whom have a similar work approach: collaborative and committed to client success. Bargmann Hendrie + Archetype, Inc. (BH+A) was hired to design two Boston offices, and the firm took these employee attributes into consideration. Having mastered a roster of high-tech clients, such as Cambridge Soft, Oracle, and IONA, as well as a bevy of institutional and advertising clients, the firm was well-equipped to handle the more than 88,000 square feet (8,175 square meters) in two locations. The design team also started the process with an "image/culture" session because this start-up enterprise wanted to define itself through words that would be consistent descriptors for simultaneous new projects. The phrases from this session incorporated into the scheme included: use of contrasting textures, professional but young, edgy and uneven.

Housed in multistory industrial buildings, the two projects are located in an urban area on the edge of the central downtown office district. In recent years, the area has been undergoing much renovation and development after years of decline. BH+A's role in this project included the rehabilitation of the buildings at 711 Atlantic Avenue and Beach Street, interior architecture, and furniture selection. The design team included: principal-in-charge Carolyn Hendri; associate-in-charge Elizabeth Tuck; Harry Hepburn, Laurel Keene, Stephen Kelley, and Brett Robillard. The client representative was

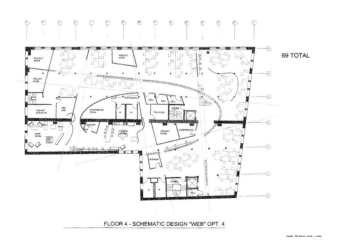

69 TOTAL

FLOOR 4 - SCHEMATIC DESIGN "WEB" OPT. 4

Pam Fuller; the MEP engineer, Shooshanian Engineering Associates, Inc.; the general contractor, Landmark Construction (Atlantic Avenue) and StructureTone, Inc. (Beach Street); and tenant project manager, Cresa Partners.

Because this start-up enterprise wanted to create spaces that reflected its work practices, which are continually evolving, the design included four priorities. The first, collaboration. "We wanted to create spaces that would invite interaction, including the most informal areas such as the kitchens, lounges, and break areas," say Hendri. Next, building a brand identity using the firm's logo (ZA4), colors, typefaces, and style to reinforce the company's essence. A sense of uniqueness that integrates distinct design features for each of the five locations. And, finally, egalitarianism. "The client wanted a non-hierarchical design solution that reflected the culture of the company," says Hendri.

Starting with a "blitz charrette" and working with phrases from the company's promotional literature such as "edgy, experimental, and unconventional," BH+A and the client developed design solutions that expressed the company's culture. The design of both spaces achieves its vitality from contrasting materials, textures, and colors while preserving and honoring the industrial qualities of the existing maple and brick as seen in the conference rooms of the Atlantic Avenue and Beach Street spaces.

A problem for both spaces was the lack of natural light. BH+A resolved this with the use of translucent screens and walls animated by low voltage, dramatic lighting, creating a glowing, luminous quality in the open, dynamic plans. Materials that were used included polycarbonate panels, acrylic panels, cold rolled steel, metal laminates, maple, Bentley carpet, and Teknion furniture systems. The wood floor at the Beach Street location is a "new" recycled floor on a plywood subfloor. The other major constraint for these projects was budget. The location was built for $35 per square foot, which by necessity included significant improvements to HVAC and electrical systems.

Zefer recently aligned itself with a select group of software and hardware vendors including Microsoft, People Soft/Vantive, Sun Microsystems, and BroadVision. As a result, the company will continue to develop and expand further. BH+A's design model was developed to carry the company through their growth spurt and beyond, with timeless planning.

Various preliminary hand sketches for the Beach Street facility.

 Top: Both spaces lacked natural light. As a solution, translucent screens and walls animated by low-voltage, dramatic lighting, create a luminous quality in the open areas and reception area of the Beach Street facility.

Bottom Left: As per the client's request, the architects wanted to create spaces that would invite interaction, including the most informal areas such as the kitchens and break areas.

Bottom Right: Both the Atlantic Avenue and Beach Street spaces use contrasting materials to preserve the industrial qualities of the existing maple and brick as seen here in the various conference rooms.

The designers used a variety of simple materials including polycarbonate panels, acrylic panels, cold rolled steel, and metal laminates.

Working with the manufacturer Teknion furniture systems, the architects managed to create workstations that satisfy the pickiest cubicle dweller.

Nestled in an unassuming office tower **in downtown** Philadelphia, **PricewaterhouseCoopers'** center for global management consulting, **The Zone,** is the result of a company **realigning its approach to client service** and partnering with

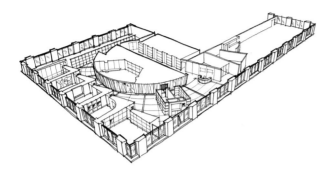

PricewaterhouseCoopers' center for global management consulting is a space that facilitates the company's high-tech approach using intense, memorable sensory impressions.

a like-minded architecture firm, Gensler, to design a space that facilitates its approach using intense, memorable sensory impressions. State-of-the-art demonstration, development, and training capabilities are housed in this single location that takes a dramatic new approach to presenting and delivering the company's global business technology solutions. Clients, who are CEOs, CFOs, CIOs, COOs, and senior business unit executives, get to "test drive" the company's talent and solutions from strategy through implementation before signing up for longer-term consulting.

From the moment visitors enter the space, they know that this is not just another software demo or sales presentation. Instantly, there is an impression, through the combination of light, sound, and video. Consultant teams physically lead clients through the company's core services; visitors learn how to use, adapt, and understand technology solutions. By designing this space for client interaction as well as solution development, the entire consulting process has been altered. Consultants don't interview clients, send them away, and then invite them back to see the software applications. Clients work through solutions with their consultants and fully understand what they will take back to their companies, building a stronger relationship along the way.

The mission of this project was to revolutionize the client interaction experience and brand the owner as the premier global provider of technology solutions. This mission branched into several goals and related design/cultural solutions. The design incorporates the most advanced technology available, including plasma screens, computer/Internet terminals, and electronic marker boards throughout the space. Fully interactive technology and videoconferencing in all areas allow for real-time links to other sites, experts, and teams. Neutral finishes and simple architecture provide a background for the business message, and color is provided by lights, multimedia, and backlit images. Reflective surfaces such as stainless steel and terrazzo intensify the effects. The space is constantly transformed through the use of sound, video, and lighting, keeping it fresh without redesign.

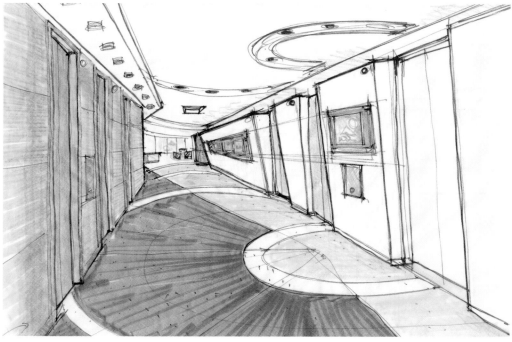

The design incorporates advanced technology, including plasma screens, computer/Internet terminals, and electronic marker boards, throughout the space.

Gensler and the client worked together to create the Industry Competency Center (ICC), which consists of four rooms that represent the firm's key global practices: Consumer & Industrial Products, Energy, Information Communications and Entertainment, and Financial Services. A fifth room was left "unbranded" to allow for future expansion of the firm's practice areas. In each room, a unique environment reflects the industry it supports. In the Consumer & Industrial Products room, metal, glass, bleached wood flooring, and furnishings reflect premier industrial design, while exposed electrical and gas conduits, meters, industrial light fixtures, and materials in their natural state adorn the Energy room, representing utilities industries. Also, technology and media content are customized to reflect the industry represented in each room.

Consultant teams, made of experts from across the firm's global practice, work in the Development Area. The aesthetic is casual and evocative of high-tech office environments, with flexible workstations that can be changed quickly for different teams. The sophisticated technology is accommodated through carefully coordinated infrastructure, wiring, and furniture. Fixed service spines provide extensive data and voice cabling, allowing for fast reconfigurations.

Making this high-powered environment more human was critical. High-tech equipment is balanced with high-touch materials like leather and wood. Convenient touch pad kiosks with Internet access in the entry and on autopoles throughout the space make it easy for clients to catch up on stock prices or communicate with their office. A radial layout is reinforced by the terrazzo pattern in the floor and ceiling design with "spokes" leading to various functional areas, resulting in intuitive meandering.

Where once PricewaterhouseCoopers used to walk one client through the door every week, the company is now hosting from three to seven. Time frames for solution development have decreased varying from three to six months, also depending on project scope, allowing faster client service and more rapid deployment of consultants to other projects. Repeat and add-on business has increased because of faster solutions development, more effective decision-making, and cost-effectiveness. And, clients simply want to return to this unique and stimulating space.

On a deeper level, the company has been pleased with how the space design and approach has had an incredible impact on their staff, company, and clients. Consultants are happier with their work experience and their ability to hit the ground running with the space and technology they need. Work practices and cultural changes enabled by the new space design are being implemented at other corporate locations. The space has fully achieved project goals for branding the firm as a problem solver and technology leader. Past spaces designed for Pricewaterhouse had a limited capacity for personal interaction, hands-on testing, and demonstrations and most of all, they couldn't exemplify the core of the company's existence: ideas. Through technology, experiential process, and hands-on sensibility, this space makes it clear what the firm is all about.

Four rooms represent the firm's key global practices. Here, exposed electrical and gas conduits, meters, industrial light fixtures, and materials in their natural state adorn the Energy room.

A critical project mandate was to make the high-powered environment more human. Thus, high-tech equipment is balanced with high-touch materials like leather and wood.

Directory of Firms and Photography

Anderson Architects
555 West 25th Street, 6th floor
New York, NY 10001
(212) 620-0996
(212) 620-5299
info@andersonarch.com
CLIENT barnesandnoble.com pp. 34-37,
<kpe> pp. 118-121, Predictive pp. 136-139
PHOTOGRAPHY Michael Moran

Bargmann Hendrie + Archetype (bh+a)
316 Summer Street
Boston, MA 02210
(617) 350-0450
(617) 350-0215
bha@bhplus.com
www.bhplus.com
CLIENT Zefer pp. 196-199
PHOTOGRAPHY Chuck Choi

Christopher Rose Architecture
21 Columbus Avenue, Suite 213
San Francisco, CA 94111
(415) 956-0788
(415) 956-5885
CLIENT ATTIK pp. 22-25
PHOTOGRAPHY Richard Barnes

D'Aquino Monaco
180 Varick Street, 4th floor
New York, NY 10014
(212) 929-9787
(212) 929-9225
MON-ARCH@Interport.net
CLIENT Eagle River Interactive pp. 74-77
PHOTOGRAPHY Rob Gray

Datum/O
368 Broadway, Suite 202
New York, NY 10013
(212) 962-3381
(212) 962-3386
www.datumzero.com
CLIENT Digital Pulp pp. 66-69
PHOTOGRAPHY Anthony Hamboussi

Emmerson Troop
8111 Beverly
West Hollywood, CA 90048
(323) 653 9763
(323) 653 5445
CLIENT Straw Dogs pp. 168-171
PHOTOGRAPHY Toshi Yoshimi

Fox & Fowle
22 West 19th Street
New York, NY 10011
(212) 627-1700
(212) 463-8716
CLIENT ClickThings pp. 54-57
PHOTOGRAPHY David Sundberg/ESTO

Freecell
586 5th Avenue, 2nd floor
Brooklyn, NY 11215
(718) 369-1617
CLIENT Liquid Design Group, pp. 122-123
PHOTOGRAPHY Mr. Means

Gensler
2500 Broadway, Suite 300
Santa Monica, CA 90404
(310) 449-5600
(310) 449-5850
CLIENT CarsDirect.com, pp. 46-49
PHOTOGRAPHY Benny Chan
Washington, DC
(202) 721-5200
(202) 872-8587
CLIENT Eisner pp. 86-89, The Zone at
PriceWaterhouseCoopers pp. 200-203
PHOTOGRAPHY Paul Warchol

Gerner Kronick + Valcarcel Architects
35 Waterside Plaza
New York, NY 10010
(212) 679-6362
(212) 679-5877
CLIENT SFX Entertainment, pp. 152-155
PHOTOGRAPHY Paul Warchol

Gould Evans Associates
3136 North 3rd Avenue
Phoenix, AZ 85013
(602) 234-1140
(602) 234-1156
www.geaf.com
CLIENT Studio at Third Avenue pp. 172-175
PHOTOGRAPHY Bill Timmerman

Hellmuth, Obata, & Kassabaum (HOK)
620 Avenue of the Americas
New York, NY 10011
(212) 741-1200
(212) 688-4846
CLIENT AT&T pp. 18-21
PHOTOGRAPHY Peter Paige

HLW
115 Fifth Avenue
New York, NY 10003
(212) 353-4600
(212) 353-4666
CLIENT Agency.com pp. 10-13
PHOTOGRAPHY Christopher Lovi

Holey Associates
2 South Park
San Francisco, CA 94107
(415) 537-0999
(415) 537-0953
mail@holeyassociates.com
CLIENT Pomegranit pp. 132-135,
Wired Digital pp. 192-195
PHOTOGRAPHY Paul Warchol

Huntsman Architectural Group
465 California Street, Suite 1000
San Francisco, CA 94104
www.HuntsmanAG.com
CLIENT Sofinnova pp. 164-167,
Wineshopper.com pp. 188-191
PHOTOGRAPHY David Wakely

Hut Sachs
414 Broadway
New York, NY 10012
(212) 219-1567
(212) 219-1677
www.hutsachs.com
CLIENT Screaming Media pp. 148-151
PHOTOGRAPHY Jeff Goldberg/ESTO

Interior Space International (ISI)
10960 Wilshire Boulevard, Suite 900
Los Angeles, CA 90024
(310) 473-5358
(310) 473-4908
CLIENT Interconnect pp. 114-117
PHOTOGRAPHY Toshi Yoshimi

KHRAS
Teknikerbyen 7
DK-2830 Virum
011 45 4585 444
011 45 4585 3615
www.khras.dk
khr@khras.dk
CLIENT Bang & Olufsen pp. 30-33
PHOTOGRAPHY Ib Sørensen, Ole Meyer

Lomar Arkitekter
8 Tobaksspinnargatan
Stockholm, Sweden SE 11736
011 08 658 10 11
011 08 658 10 12
kontoret@lomar.se
CLIENT EHPT pp. 82-85
PHOTOGRAPHY Åke E-Son Lindman Studio

Mancini Duffy
Two World Trade Center, Suite 2110
New York, NY 10048
(212) 393-0100
(212) 938-1267
www.manciniduffy.com
CLIENT Condé Nast pp. 58-61
PHOTOGRAPHY Peter Paige

Messana O'Rorke
118 West 22nd Street, 9th floor
New York, NY 10011
(212) 807-1960
(212) 807-1966
CLIENT Axis Theatre pp. 26-29
PHOTOGRAPHY Elizabeth Felicella

Morphosis
2041 Colordao Avenue
Santa Monica, CA 90404
(310) 453-2247
(310) 829-3270
Studios@morphosis.net
CLIENT SHR Perceptual Management *pp. 156-159*
PHOTOGRAPHY Farshid Assassi

NBBJ
85 Fifth Avenue, 10th floor
New York, NY 10003
(212) 924-9000
(212) 924-9292
www.nbbj.com
CLIENT eEmerge *pp. 78-81*
PHOTOGRAPHY Marjorie Fernandez

Nucreatives
42 Shelton Street
London, England WC2H 9Hz
011 44 207 379 3730
011 44 207 379 3731
CLIENT Nutopia *pp. 124-127*
PHOTOGRAPHY James Winspear

ORMS
1 Pine Street
London, England EC1R 0JH
011 44 20 7833 8533
011 44 20 7837 7575
orms@orms.co.uk
www.orms.co.uk
CLIENT Hill & Knowlton *pp. 106-109*
PHOTOGRAPHY Peter Cook

Partners by Design
213 West Institute Place, Suite 203
Chicago, IL 60610
(312) 649-111
(312) 649-0993
CLIENT Coolsavings.com *pp. 62-65*
PHOTOGRAPHY George Lambros

Pugh & Scarpa
Bergamot Station
2525 Michigan Avenue
Building F-1
Santa Monica, CA 90404
(310) 828-0226
(310) 453-9606
psk@pugh-scarpa.com
www.pugh-scarpa.com
CLIENT Click3XLA *pp. 50-53*
PHOTOGRAPHY Marvin Rand

Resolution: 4 Architecture
150 West 28th Street, Suite 1902
New York, NY 10001
(212) 675-9266
(212) 206-0944
CLIENT Thunder House *pp. 176-179*
PHOTOGRAPHY Peter Mauss/ESTO

Retail Planning Associates (RPA)
580 North 4th Street
Columbus, OH 43215
(614) 564-1000
(614) 564-1010
www.rpaworldwide.com
CLIENT Smith Bros. Hardware *pp. 160-163*
PHOTOGRAPHY Chun Y Lai

Sidnam Petrone
136 West 21st Street
New York, NY 10011
(212) 366-5500
(212) 366-6559
CLIENT America Online *pp. 14-17*
PHOTOGRAPHY Michael Moran

Space
363 West Erie Street, Suite 400
Chicago, IL 60610
www.workplayce.com
CLIENT Euro RSG Tatham *pp. 90-93,*
Upshot *pp. 180-183*
PHOTOGRAPHY Hedrich Blessing

Specht Harpman
338 West 39th Street, 10th floor
New York, NY 10018
(212) 239-1150
(212) 239-1180
CLIENT Blue Hypermedia *pp. 42-45,* Funny Garbage
pp. 102-105, Hurd Studio *pp. 110-113*
PHOTOGRAPHY Michael Moran

STUDIOS Architecture
588 Broadway, Suite 702
New York, NY 10012
(212) 431-4512
(212) 431-6042
1625 M Street, NW
Washington, DC 20036
(202) 736-5900
(202) 736-5959
CLIENT Bates *pp. 38-41*
PHOTOGRAPHY Andrew Bordwin
CLIENT RiskMetrics *pp. 140-143*
PHOTOGRAPHY Paul Warchol

The Phillips Group
11 West 42nd Street
New York, NY 10036
(212) 768-0800
(212) 768-1597
CLIENT DoubleClick *pp. 70-73*
PHOTOGRAPHY Brian Rose
CLIENT Oxygen Media *pp. 128-131*
PHOTOGRAPHY T. Whitney Cox

The Unit
Wellzeile 17
Vienna, Austria A-1010
011 43 5133007
011 43 5133008
CLIENT Kremser Bank/4 You Youth Bank *pp. 6-9*
PHOTOGRAPHY Nikolaus Korab

TVS
2700 Promenade Two
1230 Peachtree Street, NE
Atlanta, Georgia 30309
(404) 888-6600
(404) 888-6700
CLIENT Executive Presentation Theater *pp. 94-97*
PHOTOGRAPHY Brian Gassell

Ursing Architects Bureau
Munkdrogatan 8
Stockholm, Sweden 1127
011 46 8 44 00 824
011 46 8 44 00 754
www.lokaler.dn.se/entreprenorer/arkitekter
CLIENT Fluidminds *pp. 98-101*
PHOTOGRAPHY Hakansson + Mannberg

William Green & Associates
6 West 18th Street
New York, NY 10011
(212) 924-2828
(212) 924-1218
wga@interport.net
CLIENT Scient *pp. 144-147*
PHOTOGRAPHY Andrew Bordwin

William T. Georgis Architect
275 Madison Avenue, Suite 2002
New York, NY 10016
(212) 557-6577
(212) 557-6578
CLIENT Videoconferencing Office *pp. 184-187*
PHOTOGRAPHY T. Whitney Cox

About the Author

Elana Frankel, currently a senior editor at *Interior Design* magazine, has written on architecture and design for *Architectural Record, Metropolis, I.D., Grid,* and *HOME.* In addition, she is a frequent lecturer and panelist both in the United States and abroad. She resides in New York City.

Acknowledgments

I would like to thank my research assistant Pernille Pederson, the entire staff at *Interior Design* magazine; and all the architects, designers, and marketing staff who gave their time to make this book possible.